CONQUER WORRY AND ANXIETY FOR WOMEN

Anxiety Relief Techniques to Calm Your Anxious Mind and Develop Positive Habits for Self-Improvement

By Olivia Lane

Contents

Introduction

> "You must do the thing you think you cannot do."
> **- Eleanor Roosevelt.**

Anxiety isn't something that should be tolerated by those who live with it. It isn't a friend you need to make a place at the table for; it isn't a feeling you should learn to be familiar with.

The chances are that you're experiencing some level of anxiety, which is why you've reached this book. Perhaps you've been living with it for some time, or it could be new and building inside you. Either way, I know how uncomfortable it can be and how it can take over every aspect of life.

The World Health Organization (WHO) states that in 2019, 301 *million* people were living with an anxiety disorder, including a vast 58 million children and young people. These are just those who have been diagnosed.

Anxiety is a global problem, and the numbers aren't improving. I firmly believe this is because too many people learn to accept rather than challenge it. You can challenge yours, and that's why I want to work with you.

This book is home to a collection of valuable nuggets of

information alongside a modest amount of very doable activities you can tackle, one by one. That's what anxiety is about - taking everything one step at a time, but making sure you put in the effort to take *all* the steps.

Your anxiety symptoms may drain you of all your energy, but they can be reduced because your anxiety as a whole can be reduced. You've got to want to reduce it, and you also have to accept that some days are harder than others.

I believe you do it because I have seen so many others achieve their goal of a reduction in anxiety, and it has helped open numerous doors and opportunities for them. Big or small, what goals do you have that anxiety is getting in the way of?

According to Champion Health, less than 50% of people who suffer from generalized anxiety disorder access treatment or get help - that is an awful lot of people suffering in silence and the catalyst for the production of this book. If you fall into that category, having this in your hands will be priceless for you.

Modern life is evidently very hard, with more and more people struggling to juggle everything and keep anxiety, worry, and fear at bay.

As a child, I remember my own mother being around certain people and changing. She would clam up and become totally focused on just surviving the moment, and I didn't realize at the time how devastating that must have been for her. To feel as though you're constantly fighting something that only exists in your head (but is incredibly real all the same) must have taken up all her energy. I didn't know the name for it back then, but it was apparent to me she was suffering. Now I know it was the result of someone who made drastic assumptions and chose worst-case scenarios amongst people who did not want to see her thrive. I'm happy to say that she got the help she needed in later years and has her anxiety under more control.

Do you ever feel this way? It's as if something much stronger than you has taken over, and you don't know whether to fight, run away, or simply freeze on the spot? Your heart begins to race, you feel a heart palpitation, your palms become clammy. The most frustrating aspect of these symptoms is the frustration behind experiencing them, which only ignites more anxiety.

Trying to escape the strong clutches of anxiety seem impossible until you realize you're holding the bolt cutters to free yourself.

You really *are*.

I want you to see this book for what it is - a helpful guide to lead you out of the woods of worry. I'm not your doctor, and as much as I would love to be, I am not your therapist. What I *can* be, is a friendly voice that lifts you out of your concerns, and helps you see them as fixable, rather than fixed. You need strategies that are practical, and that's where I can help you.

When I think of all the well-known women in the world with anxiety, I am always brought back to Lady Gaga. Her perception of her anxiety is that in order to control it, she needs to apply strong boundaries. To overcome her own negative feelings, she learned to say no, and mean it. After some time, she started to see herself again, and eventually, she managed to shrink her anxiety to a manageable level.

This book will teach you about those boundaries Lady Gaga speaks of - and much more. It's meant to be a combination of information and activities to get you really digging into your own experience with anxiety and how new habits, thoughts, and beliefs can shape and shift your view of the mental health problems you have been living with.

You can do this too, I promise.

Anxiety builds and grows due to the negative stories you tell it and the belief behind those stories.

You can learn to stop this from happening.

Are you ready to dive in?

Chapter

1

UNDERSTANDING WORRY AND ANXIETY

Worry and anxiety present themselves in so many different ways, but more than that, they show up in various degrees of intensity.

A person who lives with anxiety can have fantastic days where symptoms appear few, far between, or not at all. Others are crippled with it, preventing them from living the day-to-day life the way they want to.

Anxiety and worry usually go hand in hand, but it is possible, in fact natural, to both worry and feel anxious from time to time. Real problems begin when both worry and anxiety are hard to either control or overcome, leading to a life half lived.

Many women I meet remember feeling anxious as a child, but they all recall, 'not having a name for it.' Having these knots in your tummy when you're little can feel trapping and not understanding why they are there. The body reacts to this by injecting more worry, creating more anxiety, and thus, the vicious cycle begins.

The fact is - it does have a name - and that name is *anxiety*.

But what exactly *is* anxiety?

What is Anxiety?

Anxiety is an emotion that we all experience. Our brain responds to stress and lets us know that there is danger afoot when the brain lets the body know something is wrong. This activates a stress hormonal response you may have heard of, called the 'fight or flight response.'

Imagine you were lost in the woods. It's getting dark, and you have no way of knowing which way is out. As the last sprinkle of daylight fades, you are left with nothing but the sound of the trees rustling in the light breeze, and the distant sound of bears. You can hear they are getting nearer to you.

Your body will respond to this by releasing hormones to help you. The adrenalin that starts pumping will give you the energy you need to run and get the heck out of there as fast as you can. It will also give you the energy you need to fight it. Do you fancy fighting a bear? Of course - you could freeze, as your entire body locks up, and you hope the bear passes you by without sight or sound.

Your body is doing what it knows how to do when there is

danger nearby. It gives you the chance to flee or fight, and helps you by releasing exactly what it needs to.

What if, though, there is no bear? What if there are no woods, no darkness, and you aren't lost?

What if you experience this same heart-pounding, panic-stricken, fight-or-flight fear every time you get stuck in traffic? Or when you go to bed at night and worry about what you must do the next day? Or when you cannot determine the moods of others? Or even sitting down and having a cup of tea?

Anxiety is a response to a situation we are either in, or imagine to be in, but those who live with it long term, are often plagued by the latter more so, because they live their lives in the future, or what could or might go wrong.

What exactly happens to the brain when you are anxious?

Three parts of your brain become involved when anxiety ignites.

1. Your frontal lobe

Your 'thinking' part of the brain. This is where you process information, read, write, and listen, and it is where the problem-solving you learn comes from. This part switches off when you're feeling overly anxious - so all reason goes out the window to prioritize your other body parts.

2. Your limbic system

Where your emotions reside - this is where your hippocampus, amygdala and hypothalamus are. It is there to help you regulate your emotions. The warning comes to you and lets you know that there is a threat and to move quickly.

3. Your brain stem

The survival part of your brain. This is the area in charge of your sleep cycle, the balance of your body temperature, breathing, and heart rate. This is the part of the brain that tells the heart to beat faster when you are anxious, so you can breathe more oxygen. It also creates fast moving limbs - so you can really run from that bear!

Anxiety disorders are a type of mental health disorder, and without treating it in some way, won't improve.

Anxiety is a little bit like an umbrella term or a general diagnosis, but there are different types of anxiety. This is where I need to state that **nobody will experience exactly the same type of anxiety.** We are all living totally different lives and experience things differently. The key is still to remember, though, that you *aren't alone* in how you feel.

- **Generalized Anxiety Disorder (or GAD)**

If you are worrying constantly, and cannot seem to get it under control, this will likely be diagnosed by a professional as GAD, especially if it has been going on for some time. It might be that you are worrying about work, money, family or friends, your health, moving house - anything really (hence the term 'generalized').

Internal stress is something you won't be able to cope well with, such as how these things are affecting you, and how you feel unable to cope with them.

- **Panic Disorders**

Panic disorder comes about where your worries and anxiety create fear and panic - even panic attacks. Avoiding certain situations will occur due to your fear of something terrible happening if you go, or if another attack will be triggered.

This creates a cycle of 'living in fear' - and your comfort zone feels smaller and smaller.

Panic attack symptoms include, but are not limited to:

- Nausea

- Chest pain

- Rapid breathing

- Shaky limbs

- Feeling faint

- Sweating

- A racing heart

- Trembling

- Hot flushes

- An out-of-body feeling - like it isn't real

- **Phobias**

Having a phobia is no joke. It can be incredibly debilitating to have such an overwhelming fear of a place, animals, a situation, or an object. More intense than fears, phobias are there because a person has an incredibly unrealistic sense of danger about their phobia. That isn't to undermine it, but it is to see that there is a root issue, rather than a direct link to safety or the risk of being in danger if exposed.

- **Social Anxiety Disorder (or SAD)**

Like any anxiety, social anxiety can make it really hard to find your day-to-day routine. It can be distressing to have a fear of social situations, especially when you know you ought to be doing things to help change this.

Social anxiety usually begins in the teenage years, and for some, it can get better, but for others, not so much.

How Does Anxiety Affect Our Lives?

If you were to fall and sprain your ankle, you'd likely head to your nearest health center and get some professional help or advice. Have you ever been asked by a doctor to describe your pain out of ten? It's a common way for them to understand your physical level of discomfort, but what about mental discomfort?

Anxiety, like all mental health disorders, should be treated this way too. There is a scale, and some people may only be sitting on 1 or 2, whilst others regularly sit somewhere between 7 and 8, or even higher.

It doesn't matter how big or small the anxiety is - it still affects lives, and it will probably be affecting your life, or someone you know dearly.

Wherever you sit on the scale, you will experience anxiety both in your body and in your mind. It can also affect your journey of life.

If you have a phobia of flying, you'll find it extremely difficult, if not impossible, to go on a plane. If you have a phobia of heights, you won't want to be doing much involving being high up. That might stop you from working in a certain building, so you might miss out on jobs, visit tourist attractions with your family or friends, or even just do something because you can.

Anxiety holds people back in so many ways, and being held back only adds to the shame and frustration you could feel about your own anxiety. Knowing you *can* do these things, but your anxiety prevents you from feeling like you're constantly stuck and you don't know how to get out. A step further from that is actually adjusting to your fears and phobias and living your entire life around them.

My very best friend has a brother who got married in Cyprus. It was in the heat of late July, and the package included a nice meal for the guests (limited to close family only) and a general, intimate celebration of his life with his new wife.

She was obviously asked to go, but her fear of flying stopped her. Not only did she miss out on a beautiful holiday, but she missed her brother's wedding. Still, her phobia was bigger than attending the nuptials, and so she missed out. Through many tears and feelings of guilt and embarrassment, she had to hear about it and see it on social media instead of being there.

Anxiety gets under people's skin, and takes root. The more they try to ignore it or even bow down to it, the harder it gets to truly shake off the worry and live lives that match their values, goals, and aspirations.

Effects of anxiety on the body can include problems with your:

- **Digestive system**

- **Cardiovascular system**

- **Immune system**

- **Nervous system**

- **Respiratory system**

Physical symptoms that can have an effect on your body can be:

- **Abdominal pain**

- **Chest pain**

- **Fatigue**

- **Insomnia**

- **Headaches**

- **Muscle pains and tension**

These symptoms can affect your life and the way you perform day-to-day tasks.

What is Worry?

Worry is a cognitive and emotional state characterized by the anticipation of potential future problems or uncertainties. It involves thinking about negative outcomes and possible threats, often accompanied by feelings of unease or fear. While worry is a normal part of human experience and can serve a protective function by helping us plan and prepare for challenges, excessive or chronic worrying can contribute to anxiety.

Worry can contribute to anxiety in several ways.

Cognitive Processes:

Worry involves any or all kinds of repetitive and intrusive thoughts about potential future threats. When these thoughts become excessive and uncontrollable, they can lead to blurred thinking or perception, such as catastrophic thinking, where the worst-case scenarios are imagined and almost brought to life in your mind. This only reinforces and intensifies your worry.

Emotional Response:

Worry is also often accompanied by emotional distress, including fear, apprehension, and tension. This emotional response can trigger physiological reactions, such as increased heart rate, muscle tension, and restlessness, contributing to the overall experience of anxiety, all similarly to anxiety.

Uncertainty and Lack of Control:

Worry is often driven by a desire to gain a sense of control over future events that feel uncertain to you. However, excessive worry can lead to heightened uncertainty because you may become hyper-focused on potential negative outcomes that are totally out of your control. This only adds fuel to the fire of anxiety. Chapter 3 goes into this in far more detail, but knowing this about worry is a great place to start.

Negative Reinforcement:

If you start to worry, there could be a slight temporary relief from anxiety by mentally preparing for potential threats. Have you ever gone over potential scenarios in your mind, or conversations you imagine having in a situation you're thinking of? This temporary relief can reinforce the habit of worrying, making it more difficult to break your own pattern of worry, and will only either develop or maintain your current worry levels.

*

Worry is more specific than anxiety. You can pick something you feel overly concerned about, such as which bus you need to take on a route that is unfamiliar. It might get stuck in your mind until the day of travel arrives, but anxiety would cover the entire journey. What might go wrong? What if I miss said bus? What if the bus breaks down and I'm late?

As your worries become thoughts, anxiety affects both body *and* mind.

Worry is rooted in reality, but anxiety lives and thrives in catastrophic thoughts - or those worst-case-scenarios I previously mentioned.

A worry will also be a little like a butterfly, flitting past your line of sight, whereas anxiety is more like the air around you - a constant. If you are worried, you'll unlikely be kept up at night, into the wee small hours wondering what you are going to do. Your focus will not be shifted from everything to this one particular thought, but anxiety will and can encompass your entire mind, and leave you with very little room to breathe on its worst days.

Benefits of Overcoming Anxiety

There could never be *disadvantages* to overcoming anxiety, but it's safe to say your own life without these levels of worry and fear would be drastically different for the better. That shouldn't be something that makes you feel more helpless or give you the 'This will never be me' attitude because it can always be you.

Overcoming anxiety isn't something that will happen overnight, but it can and will happen for you. If you have difficult days, remember that they will become fewer and farther between as you move through your journey, and you will gain strength every step of the way.

Those who have anxious predispositions will always find worry their first port of call in life, and that may be something that never goes away. Still, you *can* view those worries as emotions, rather than real causes for concern to the point where your anxiety takes over.

Overcoming anxiety can offer so many benefits, whether they be physical, emotional or social, and can lead to the following benefits:

Improved Mental Health:

One of the main benefits of overcoming anxiety is how rested your mind feels. Anxiety disorders can significantly impact how you think, making it challenging to concentrate or make decisions properly. Overcoming it can help you regain mental clarity and feel as though your mind has space again.

Enhanced Emotional Stability:

Anxiety can unlock intense and overwhelming emotions. When fear, worry, or anticipation rear their heads, you can find ways to quash them. This will bring your stability levels way back to where they should be on a regular basis, and take away all that unnecessary intensity.

Improved Physical Health:

Overcoming anxiety can lead to a reduction in stress-related physiological responses. That horrible racing heart you feel when you sit down to relax but can't because of unspecified concerns whirring around in your head can be controlled, but it's finding what works for you. Remember - there is something that works for everyone, you just have to find it.

Enhanced Relationships:

Anxiety can sadly strain relationships because communication can become lost, or emotions can become distorted. It's tricky, and tensions can rise if you are the one with anxiety, or if you live with someone with anxiety, because one person will feel helpless from time to time. Overcoming anxiety will allow you to engage more fully in your relationships and bring them back to where they should be.

Increased Productivity and Achievement:

Anxiety can get in the way of productivity or even things you want to achieve simply by setting up camp in the middle of your metaphoric path. You can sit there and observe it, or you can overcome it. One will help, and one will hinder your progress. You will be able to channel your energy far better if you choose to overcome it, leading to brand-new and exciting goals for yourself.

Greater Life Satisfaction:

Do you want a life limited by anxiety? Your experiences and personal growth both want you to be free, but there are obstacles to overcome first. Overcoming anxiety opens up opportunities for you, no matter how big or small they may be. Nobody expects or imagines you to want to travel the world and face all your fears at once, but even going to a new town or applying for that job you like the look of can be a good place to start. What could life bring you?

Enhanced Coping Skills:

Overcoming anxiety often includes the development of effective coping mechanisms and resilience. If you successfully manage anxiety, you can begin to learn valuable skills for handling future situations that would have previously left you floorless with fear.

Improved Sleep:

Anxiety *will* play havoc with your sleep patterns. Whether that be falling asleep, staying asleep, or experiencing light sleep that doesn't feel as if you've slept a wink. Overcoming anxiety can give you improved quality of sleep, which will then give you a better day when you wake.

Imagine Your Life - Anxiety Free

So, what would your life look like without a smidge of anxiety in it?

Where would your dreams take you? What job would you have? Where would you go on vacation? Would you have better friends? Can you finally make a start on that hobby you've been previously self-conscious about? Would your new, worry-free life take you in a new career direction? Would that one thing you've always wanted to do suddenly become achievable?

If your dream was to visit the orange valleys of Seville in Spain, but you never *dreamed* you'd be able to do it due to your fear of flying, imagine for a moment that flying was just like hopping in a cab to get from one destination to another. This *can* be you.

You're on the plane, enjoying a nice cold drink, and looking out the window at this beautiful planet from above. You see towns, villages, lakes - you name it - and you bask in the glory. It's all there for you to explore. It has waited for you all this time, and finally you are going places.

You arrive in Spain and are greeted by golden sunshine and warm temperatures. Before you know it, you are on your way to your accommodation. You drive past the rolling hills and sunken valleys, all adorned with the vibrant oranges of the world-famous fruits, and you can smell the citrus in the air.

You're there. Your dream has come true. You're living the life you dreamed of, and you feel luckier than ever.

This could be you, you know.

Nothing is impossible.

Activity

For a moment, I want you to think deeper into your life and what you want from it.

If anxiety was vastly under control in your own body and mind, or gone completely, where would you put your imagination?

For 15 minutes, I would like you to think about 5 questions about your life that you want to improve. *Where would I love to go traveling? What is my dream job?* are good questions to start with if you are unsure, but it must have an answer that isn't limited by your anxiety.

Find a cozy spot, with some nice, calm lighting, and take yourself to a solace that only exists in your mind, but travel there well.

Write each question down, with space to include your answer under each one.

What would you do if you were not bound by fear?

What do you see in your fear-free life?

Who are you with when you see your dreams come true?

What do you hear? What do you smell?

Do you feel free? Happy? Light?

You can unlock the doors and windows that you've kept closed. It is possible to overcome the fears that are holding you back, but with guidance and empathy, we can work on your healing journey together, as we turn each page.

Chapter

2

ANXIETY TRIGGERS

Anxiety triggers can be anything, from a certain smell to a certain sound. Excessive usage of alcohol might bring back terrible memories for you, or a certain place you went on holiday could make you feel as though you are reliving a past holiday from hell. Perhaps if you were neglected as a child a lot, an unanswered text could be all it takes to trigger your anxiety.

Other examples of triggers can be:

- Being rejected or let down

- Arguments

- The anniversary of a death, loss or traumatic event

- Being judged

- The news

- Physical injury or illness

- Being touched without permission

- Loud noises

When you experience a trigger, the part of your brain that remembers it becomes stimulated. It then leaves you feeling very alert, and never for good reason. This trigger will then activate your anxiety and make it feel ten times worse.

Your triggers might come as a kind of shock or surprise to people around you, who simply aren't aware of what struggles you face internally, but they are still justified to you.

Triggers aren't universal - they aren't going to be the same from one person to the next, because everybody who lives with anxiety experiences it in their own way. It wouldn't be fair to assume two friends, both with anxiety, would find the same things separately triggering; in fact, two friends with anxiety might even find ways to help each other through their triggers.

If you have anxiety, the likelihood is that you will have more than one trigger, you may even have several, but for many, including those with triggers, can suffer with a panic attack, or a sharp rise in anxious feelings and emotions for no reason - totally out of the blue.

Self-reflection is a huge part of the healing process when one is dealing with large amounts of anxiety in their lives. Triggers, at the time, feel like they are 'sent to try us' - they can come out of nowhere, and often do, because ultimately, triggers can appear anytime. It's a little like being out on a glorious sunny day, and then experiencing a sudden downpour, and it leaves people who have those triggers feeling even more on edge, or the thought of, 'what could go wrong today?'

Unexpected Events

The key message in any unexpected event is that it is what it is - unexpected. Anxiety revolves around looking at the future and determining what is going to happen, and worrying about it. In fact,according to the World Health Organization, an estimated *4%* of the global population are currently experiencing some anxiety, which makes it the most common mental health disorder there is. The future feels like something anxiety sufferers have control of, so they try to do so, without success, and that lack of control leads to simply *not knowing* what is going to happen.

This is incredibly frustrating for people who like to plan, and know, and be in the present moment. As they try to plan to the smallest detail, things will inevitably not go their way, and that is the very moment a person can be triggered.

Unexpected events are unsettling because the anxious mind assumes it to be a threat to safety. Think about it, if your boss emailed you and asked you to go and see them when you next get a chance, your immediate thoughts could include:

'Oh my goodness, what have I done wrong?'

'I have obviously made a huge error.'

'Has someone complained about me?'

'Am I going to lose my job?'

But it doesn't stop there, as the anxious mind gears up for further threat:

'How will I pay my bills?'

'What will happen if I can't pay my rent?'

'What if I don't have anywhere to live?'

'I'm going to lose everything.'

These thoughts and assumptions are triggered from one email, for unknown reasons. It is the negative impact the email would have on someone living with anxiety that causes this catastrophic thought process, and we will delve into that in far more detail in chapter 3.

Sometimes, things don't go the way we thought or planned, and when that happens, it can feel, for those who live with anxiety, as though everything is falling apart. In truth, unexpected events are unavoidable. In fact, one key thing to really help you along your journey is to think of this:

Anxiety is about worrying what the future holds, but if you really knew what the future held, would it make you feel any better?

This is a question I heard my friend say to her daughter, who has anxiety. Initially, her daughter said, *yes, absolutely, I would feel better!* After a moment to reflect on what that would mean, she decided that, in fact, she didn't feel she would have any less of a settled mind if she had insight into the future because the future can bring anything.

It's okay to find unexpected events a cause for concern, further worry or anxiety. When plans change, or something happens that you weren't prepared for, it can make anyone feel uncomfortable, but that is where there is room for adaptation, and with that initially comes acceptance of change.

New Phase of Life

How do you feel when you think of the dreaded C word?

Change.

Many people make the mistake of thinking that life never changes and that we are destined to live out each day the same as the last. Many actually find comfort in keeping their routines as consistent as possible so as not to ignite any anxiety trigger within them, but we all know life throws curveballs our way. We have no control over it, and that fact alone is enough to further ignite the anxiety in the already anxious mind.

New phases in life can appear when we know its coming, or when we are totally unprepared. Think about the last time things really changed for you, such as discussing moving house (planned change) , or a relationship ending that was not your decision (surprise change). You can see how anything resulting in change can leave someone triggered by the panic it injects.

Questions in your mind will begin to paint a picture of your future before you've even got there. They can include:

'What will I do now?'

'How will it all work out?'

'How am I going to cope?'

'What if it all goes wrong?'

'My life is changing so quickly, why can't I just roll with it?'

*

New phases are welcomed much better when you can start to learn to accept that change is inevitable, but that doesn't automatically make that change *negative*. Embracing change is extremely difficult for those of anxious tendencies. It isn't as easy as flicking a switch or simply 'deciding not to be worried about something,' after all, how many times has your anxiety appeared, and somebody has told you, 'not to worry.' It's frustrating, to say the least! If only that were possible so quickly. The good news is that it *is* still possible, just not at such lightning speed.

Past Experiences

Our past remains active in our minds because our memory keeps those moments alive - whether they are good or bad. Unpacking the past can be painful if what happened would rather be forgotten, but sometimes it isn't possible to keep past experiences locked up, especially if a present trigger allows it to float back to the surface.

Past experiences in fact, can be so traumatic that even remembering them can incite a wide range of anxious symptoms, both mental and physical, which are all down to an element of 'reliving what once was.'

If a relationship you thought would last forever ended in your past, and you eventually found somebody who you loved and trusted again, you'd probably feel over the moon. If your new partner takes you to the same restaurant that was the venue for the end of your past relationship as a surprise, it'll be enough to take you right back to that time, and throw all the worry and pain at you that you felt that day.

Similarly, if you went for a job interview that you desperately wanted to succeed in, and you didn't, that might prevent you from putting yourself back onto the career market again, leaving you to only miss out on opportunities by default. Receiving an email or letter to say that you have been shortlisted for an interview could be just enough to trigger all that self-doubt you once felt, leaving you no other option but to decline.

These triggers aren't your fault. They don't define you. The past, equally, does not define you. You, like everyone, have lived a life that hasn't always gone your way. It has thrown events your way that you wish you could forget, but your brain refuses to. That's because one of the brain's many jobs is to protect us from threats.

My sister burned her hand when she was five. We were at our aunt's house, and she had a beautiful floor lamp, and it filled the room with a comforting, warm glow. My sister was mesmerized by it and kept trying to put her hand near the light bulb. "Stop that, you'll burn your fingers," my aunt said, several times in fact. Did that stop my sister? Nope! Her hand clasped the light bulb fully, and she let out an almighty scream that my then eleven-year-old self still recalls.

The temptation was just too much for her, and after a visit to the emergency care center and a time later, the burns subsided and her hand returned to normal. That didn't stop her from regretting her decision, and she was never tempted to do that again (thank goodness!)

What the brain did was store the memory of her burning herself, and created a reason for her not to do it again - because she would hurt herself again.

The brain protects. It keeps hold of situations that threatened us, and uses those past experiences to remind us in our present moment to not repeat them.

That's all well and good when it comes to actual health and safety, but what if you had a panic attack at the supermarket during the holiday customer rush? You might have come over feeling very warm and trapped in a place you wish you could just run out of (with all your shopping paid for, of course). As the panic sets in, of course, the brain automatically looks for a way out. However the event ends, it ends with you no longer being in there and returning to a calmer state of mind.

What happens now, though? Is the supermarket a place you now avoid at all costs because you had a panic attack? Was the supermarket the reason, or was it because you felt overwhelmed in a situation you couldn't immediately escape?

The brain is unable to differentiate, it will just remember how you felt, and where you felt it, so it will tell you that going there again is probably a bad idea. What if it doesn't stop there though? What if it tells you that any shop should be avoided, or any place that's likely to be warm or busy?

Where could it end?

The brain keeps track of everything you do, even if you don't consciously recall it.

PTSD (Post Traumatic Stress Disorder) is a disorder associated with anxiety that involves reliving trauma from your past. It's probably familiar to you, because of its widely known association to veterans returning from war. Over recent years, PTSD has also been recognized, very fairly so, in those who have experienced extreme stress or trauma in other ways, such as perhaps involving a death, a serious injury, some assault, or abuse.

It is said that by the age of 18, 1 in 4 people who have

experienced trauma will have developed PTSD. It affects millions of people all over the world, with the World Health Organization (WHO) declaring that approximately 3.6% of the global population experienced some PTSD in the last year alone. Those are the people who have been diagnosed, so the number is likely to be higher, but translates to around 250 million people. That's almost *three times* the UK population. This is such a high amount of people who feel alone, but indeed are not. They will be reliving experiences that were unsettling to them, and even developing strategies that help them avoid anything similar to this in their present lives. They will be constantly on guard for triggers that will send them back to their trauma. It could be a sight, a sound, a smell, a feeling, a place - and often they will overly avoid to try and keep themselves safe from further threat.

Do you think about your past much, or has your constant fear of reliving something you'd rather not, taken over your life to the point where you change your routine to accommodate it? It isn't uncommon, and you aren't weird or crazy at all. You're perfectly normal to want to shield yourself from what caused you great pain.

It's important to have a support system in place to help you overcome the acute symptoms experienced from PTSD, and luckily there are many therapists with training in it to help guide you through your emotions and experiences. It is well worth investing in one if you are ready to explore it more detail.

Unhealthy Relationships

We can all agree that when it comes to relationships, the healthier the better. If a relationship isn't healthy and you are of an anxious predisposition, you are going to feel those anxiety symptoms skyrocket all the while the relationship is still alive.

The only way to know if you are in an unhealthy relationship is to reflect upon it, and you, since it began, and if it *isn't,* it will trigger your anxiety because it will incite worry and negative thoughts into you.

Love is supposed to be a good, positive thing, and we all need it in our lives. If relationships, no matter who you are with, aren't going as well as you want them to, then it can have a huge impact on your mental health, and certainly anxiety levels.

- **Friends**

When things don't seem to be going well with your friends, you could experience things such as silent treatment, little thought or regard, reduced contact, or people making plans without you. Those are three things strongly linked to anxiety triggers. Thoughts of not being good enough, catastrophizing, pulling yourself further and further away from socializing with them, making you feel panicky and alone and setting off a number of symptoms in your own anxiety that you experience when you feel dynamics shift and change.

Unhealthy relationships with friends can leave a person feeling like they are doing all the hard work or being a bit of a doormat to their friends. It's important to have balance in your friendship circles because friendships are about respect and loyalty. Anything that feels off will only make you question your self-worth, which will lead to anxiety triggers. You deserve great friends, and you should always believe that when you are going through a bad time with yours.

- **Family**

Family, we are told, is incredibly important. 'Family should stick together, blood is thicker than water, when all else fails, turn to family.' Well, number one, we aren't all blessed with the perfect family, and many people in fact are out of touch with some, if not all of their own family, for reasons personal and justified to them.

What happens when there are unhealthy dynamics with a family? Well, they can trigger anxiety without a doubt. The last people who should be neglecting your relationship are members of your family, but believe me, it is far more common than you think, and you *can* overcome the triggers that this type of dynamic brings.

It is becoming more and more widely talked about now, but the idea that there are 'toxic' family members out there is getting a lot of people talking about how they realized, what it was doing to their mental health and anxiety levels, and how the toxicity affected their moods, thoughts and feelings about themselves, and more direct symptoms, such as their stress levels or even how they slept.

You need to do what's right for you in these situations, and if that even starts with the awareness of your triggers, then you are a step closer to overcoming them.

- **Romantic Partners**

Romantic partners - or people we mutually *choose to be with* - should be last on the list of people who trigger your anxiety intentionally or repeatedly. It's important to be clear here that when you enter a romantic relationship, the other person isn't going to know everything about you immediately. There is a lot of 'getting to know you' at the start, and even as relationships progress, and sometimes you may be triggered harmlessly.

To be repeatedly triggered, with the other person knowing they are hurting you or causing your anxiety to rise, is not healthy. In fact, it is the opposite of healthy, but often people stay for love.

Love isn't enough in many cases. You also need mutual respect and understanding, and whilst mistakes happen, and apologies can be made, they are also learned from and not repeated, because that is where harm becomes intentional rather than accidental.

If you feel worthless, you are going to be hard-pressed to find somebody who makes you feel worthy in the long term. You must always love yourself wholly before you can allow yourself to love another. Valuing yourself as you are, rather than who you want to be, is a step toward finding someone else who can do the same.

Once you find a healthy relationship, you will find there is room to talk and open up to your partner, and those triggers you find you have, can either be overcomed with their help, or lessened due to the support they give you to heal them.

- **Work Colleagues**

Work is the trickiest of all relationships to find your way around, because you are in a professional environment that must allow for you also to be professional. However, there are times when anxiety triggers can manifest in the workplace, and that is due to people or situations out of your control.

Someone got that promotion over you, you have to go and close a contract on that client you find cold and uncaring, there is a lot of sickness, so your workload becomes three times as much, or you are repeatedly asked to work late to get a project done. The list of work related issues that can trigger anxiety is neverending, and what might not trigger one person, could be your main trigger.

If there are unhealthy relationships at work that are causing you stress, where you don't feel appreciated, or where things are getting to be too much, then of course, you are going to feel those triggers rise, and that can give way to you finding work to be the place you want to avoid. It's the main cause for people being off sick long term - stress.

*

The brain is excellent at remembering everything in some way. If something negative happens to you, it will store what it can from that moment in order to protect you in the future. This can be sights, sounds, smells, textures - anything.

If you feel triggered, it is important to consciously remind yourself that you are in the present moment, where what happened to you before, has been and gone.

Look down on your situation, and see yourself now detached from it.

Remind yourself how safe you are.

Accept that you are feeling this way and that it will pass.

Meditate - there really is no better way than to gain mental clarity and distance from the mental chaos triggers give us.

Triggers will always be moments of time you'd rather forget, attempting to come back and remind you of them. Remembering your strength, and all the ways you can overcome them, will help you get to the place you want to be, rather than remain at the place you feel most stuck.

Chapter

NEGATIVE THOUGHTS AS THE CULPRIT

I am sure you are all familiar with negative thoughts, because you're likely as an anxiety sufferer to have them, perhaps even frequently. Negative thoughts serve a useless purpose:

Negative thoughts increase fear, worry or/and anxiety.

Anxiety and negative thoughts go hand in hand, because the worry you feel about your negative thoughts only serve to cause more anxiety. That cycle can go round and round, and is so difficult to break. You probably know that already, because you are living your own experiences.

Your brain is able to do so many things that it's actually impossible to count the exact number. One thing it does well is trigger negative thoughts when you are feeling anxious, and even sometimes when everything feels great, and you're having a day free from worry, something can crop up in your mind, usually a single thought, and that's all it takes for negative thoughts to spill over.

Negative thoughts lead to the mind making so many mistakes, and they make people with anxiety feel like they have no option but to think about them, and even worse, believe them. The trick of the mind is just that, because with enough training and work, you can change how you think and feel, and those negative thoughts, even if they do reappear, will be thoughts you can dismiss, rather than eat into.

Another term for negative thinking is known as *cognitive distortion*, which ultimately makes you think more negatively than is real and around you. The more cognitive distortions you experience, the more negative thoughts you are going to experience.

When you get stuck in that negative pattern of thought, positive thinking feels like it is well out of your reach, and it will lead to you wishing you could control things you simply cannot. What the brain *does* forget is that you *can* still control certain things, but more about that later.

Focusing on What is Out of Your Control

Focusing on what is out of your control leads to disappointment and very high levels of frustration. Why is it that our minds take us to the things we cannot even touch, let alone control?

You can remember a time this recently happened to you. Were you stuck in traffic, wanting the cars to evaporate so you could get out of the queue? What about a special birthday coming up, and you become hyper-focused on the weather, getting stressed and anxious that it won't be a clear day for you? Believe it or not, these are all reasons why people *do* feel their anxiety levels increase, and certainly ways in which negative thoughts can be blamed on increasing anxious thoughts. The focus on what should be, rather than what is, is only going to lead you down a very long road of disappointment.

A good tip to cope with things you can't control is looking at your mindset

Some examples of things you can't control are:

- **How other people think**

As much as you'd like to, other people are their own person, with their own thoughts and minds.

- **The past**

Changing the past wouldn't necessarily make the present moment any better , yet somehow we become fixated on wishing we could go back and redo something differently.

- **The what-ifs**

What if - the worst type of conflict you can give your brain. Creating an entire scenario to suit you is dangerous because it isn't real. Don't get caught up in thinking about what if; if you do, remember where you are in this moment, and try to stay mindful.

- **The weather**

Wouldn't it be lovely! The weather can be a cause for concern for people with anxiety, especially if they need to make a trip or if an event is planned. To be fixated on the weather, and any weather warnings is handy in everyday life, but it is important to remember you can't change it.

- **The news**

The news is one of the main catalysts of worry for people with anxiety. The world can seem as though it's falling apart, and good news is few and far between. Much of it is to inject worry into us, so we can respond in a certain way, and most of all, news is incredibly divisive not just with society, but in your mind as well.

You are not responsible for everything you think. Learning to recognize that is a really crucial step forward, and going a step further to understand how your negative thoughts can be both unhelpful and irrational will help you cope with them better. Eventually, you might even laugh at your negative thoughts, because you will grow so accustomed to challenging them, rather than accepting them as a form of reality.

I delve into the mindset further on in the chapter.

Activity

I want you to think about a time where you have focused so much on what you cannot control, that it has caused you physical and mental anxiety.

Grab a pen, and write down what your memories are of this moment, trying to capture the emotions that were going through your mind.

Did they create physical panic, as well as mental distress?

How did your thoughts form a pattern that led to your anxiety at this time?

What habits created those patterns?

Write down as much as you can, and get to know how your thoughts around control, or lack thereof, contributed to your worry.

It is in doing this on a regular basis, you can start to see, on paper, how not having control is a huge part of anxiety, but how you can change them and climb out of the habit of doing so, can save you.

Unhelpful beliefs and interpretation

Anxiety isn't about purposely thinking thoughts that are unhelpful, and heading towards incorrect interpretations of what we experience. Nobody with anxiety wakes up and consciously thinks, 'I know! I'm going to think of some of the most unhelpful things I can and make myself feel even worse than I do.' It wouldn't make sense, would it?

Unhelpful beliefs won't move you forward in your journey, all they do is hold you back and keep you feeling pained and worried.

I wonder if you thought about it, could you think of one or two beliefs you have that aren't helpful to you? Common ones are the belief that somebody isn't clever enough to go for a job they would actually love to do, so they never even bother applying for it. In not applying, they will never know either way, so it almost feeds the belief that they wouldn't get it.

Another common unhelpful belief is that you need to be better. This is the one unhelpful belief I hear about mostly because it is something we, as women, find ourselves faced with frequently. Low self-worth comes from a strong and rooted place of insecurity within a lot of women, and that can be due to past negative experiences that they just aren't over yet. Moving on from pain doesn't mean the wounds have healed, and often, if one is in an anxious state of mind, that pain only reinforces the belief that they weren't good enough in the first place. Good enough for the job, the man, the *'anything.'*

When you need help to believe or interpret something, there are several things that are likely to happen.

- **Jumping to conclusions**

Jumping to conclusions is an irrational way of very quickly assuming we know what other people are thinking, or what they are going to do. We base our own anxiety on what the next step is, and often, as jumping to conclusions goes, the anxiety in the person jumping gets it wrong. We might see or hear something, then create a story about it in our mind. From that, our anxiety forms a conclusion all by itself. Basing a conclusion on a story we created ourselves is fairly dangerous – we are working all by ourselves to start and complete something that essentially doesn't even exist.

Imagine you are trying to fall asleep, and you worry that you won't be able to do so. In your mind, you know you have something important to do the next day, and you tell yourself that if you don't sleep, you won't be able to do it. People will be disappointed with you. You'll let them down, and they won't ask you to do it again. You might even lose friends over it, or worse, your job if it's career-related. It's no use. It's now 3am and you *know* you won't sleep – so it's safe to say, tomorrow is now today, and it's all going to go drastically wrong.

Ultimately, you *cannot* predict what is going to happen in the future., but your worry can keep you from thinking about it rationally. It can be tricky believing that, though.

- **Black and white thinking**

Wrong, right, up, down, yes, no, bad, good. Are there ever any other options? Yes, there are thousands, but the anxious minded person will only feel or see one of two extremes, and that is a really unhelpful way of looking at the world and everything you experience in it.

- **Labeling**

Labeling yourself or anybody else is unhelpful in the sense that it gives you a fixed view on what or whom you're labeling. It creates a stagnant view, which is deemed to be inflexible, and a label sticks. When something sticks, it's incredibly hard to get unstuck. There are so many descriptive words or thoughts that can flow freely and prevent the concept of labeling altogether, which is a far more helpful state of mind to be in.

- **All or nothing**

All or nothing thinking is not how we should be living our lives. We shouldn't give 100% or zero, nor should we think like that. Some days, you might only be running on 65%, and that's okay. Nobody is putting pressure on you to always be the best at everything except you. This type of pressure can lead to extortionate levels of stress, and with stress comes more anxiety, panic and worry. It's the same for the zero days.

- **Personalizing**

When you automatically blame yourself for everything that goes wrong, you are shifting the blame from every other exterior possibility. That's not to say you should equally always be pointing outwardly, but call a spade a spade, and only look at yourself when you genuinely need to. If you continue to take on all the responsibility for everything all of the time, you are going to end up burned out and more anxious than ever.

How you interpret something is personal to you, and not necessarily fact. Negatively interpreting is associated with anxiety, because it leaves room for ambiguity. In other words - 'not knowing' increases levels of anxiety, which only allows minds to turn to assumptions, predictions, jumping to conclusions, and all of the above.

Activity

Black-and-white thinking can feel so drastic when we tell the stories to ourselves, but what if you were to imagine you were talking to a friend instead?

1. When you feel a thought pulling you in two contrasting thought processes, ask yourself what you'd say if it were a friend having these thoughts or beliefs.

2. Talk out loud, or journal what you would say, and in what situation for a few minutes, if it helps you see or hear your thoughts clearer.

3. Reflect on how different you would talk to your friend, as opposed to how you talk to yourself.

4. Using what you have learned, you can start applying your knowledge in *your* moments of black or white thinking.

This is a very popular activity that therapists like to offer as advice to their patients who suffer with bouts of black or white thinking - and could come in very handy for you too.

Predict the Worst / Focus on the Extreme

Assumptions are a one-way road to assuming the worst. If you think about your own anxiety, how many times do your assumptions lead you to a good place? Likely almost never!

To the non-anxious mind, assumptions are mostly harmless. The brain always tries to guess what's going to happen next, because it wants to care for you, but the *anxious* mind can and will take it to the next level.

If you have anxiety, you'll be very familiar with what it means to predict the worst. It is your brain's way of saying, 'I must do what I can to protect you, and so I will think of the worst thing that can happen, and prepare you for it.'

This is a negative thing for the brain to be able to do, but it actually thinks that it's doing you a favor by looking after you, and preparing you.

How is it preparing you though?

The prediction comes into your mind, and your body immediately responds to it. What does it do? It runs the same pattern system. Pupils dilate, heart starts to race - your body gets ready for your worst case scenario to come to life.

These thoughts are catastrophic, as well as irrational. Your body stays in that fight-or-flight mode we talked about previously, and it never really leaves. Long term, this type of thinking is enough to make anybody feel totally exhausted.

When you get into this type of negative thought pattern, it can be so hard to break, because it just becomes a part of who you are, but who you are doesn't have to be this stressed, worried person. Underneath all of the anxiety, you are still wonderful, and you are worthy of living life to the fullest you know how.

Anxiety makes that assumption really easy, but more than that, the assumption itself, brought on by your anxiety, feeds *more* anxiety. This will impact your actions. Do you distance yourself now from the person you originally text? Does it make you not want to reach out again? Those assumptions take over, and it's usually due to misinterpreting what has happened, with the help of very unhelpful assumptions.

Not assuming the worst is a real challenge. Every part of your mind will want to stick with what's familiar to it, but the way you can overcome that is to be aware that your mind likes what it knows, whether what it knows is healthy and helpful or not.

Activity

It's time to challenge your assumptions.

These steps will help you begin to overcome the assumptions you have, and help turn your negative thoughts into new habits that help ease your anxiety.

1. Find an anxious thought that you have had in the past, or frequently have.

2. When you have the thought in mind, think about the thoughts

they then create.

3. Be honest with yourself. "Are these thoughts accurate? What evidence do I have to confirm that? What might another possible explanation be?

4. Explore those other options, and then look into the thought processes behind them.

5. Remember that you carry anxious traits, and that sometimes this does happen. Be kind to yourself here, and remember that your assumptions aren't facts.

6. Notice how your wrong assumptions based on the previous chapter has led you to a point where you can think differently now. In this short space of time, you have begun to grow and identify how these assumptions that trigger your anxiety develop, and that now you are in the driving seat for *real change.*

It's challenging, and your mind will likely try to flip you back to your assumptions, but this is an activity you can do whenever you receive an assumption, and how you can change that habit.

Paying Too Much Attention or Suppression

Your energy goes where your attention takes root. Think about driving a car. You need energy for that, and you need to be aware. Having both will allow you to start the car, and drive the route you desire, in order to get to your destination. Happy days, I hear you say.

What about when your attention is on your anxiety? Even if you aren't feeling any anxious symptoms, your mind automatically drifts to why. Why do I have this? Why can't I seem to control it? Why can't I get rid of it?

Your focus on your anxiety *draws* your attention toward it like a moth to a flame.

I can't stress this enough:

The more you focus on your anxiety, the stronger it will get.

Trying to *not* feel anxious might seem like a great idea, and of course, the aim is to reduce your symptoms, but in consciously willing it to go away, you're still feeding it and giving it the time and energy it needs to continue to grow.

It's hard to stop thinking about something though, I understand that. If someone said to me, 'do *not* think of a red bus for a whole minute,' my mind, like everyone else's, will go straight to a mental picture of a great big, shiny red bus.

My thought would be, 'Well, I want to get rid of this image as quickly as possible.' But I can't do that whilst saying, 'Don't think of the red bus, don't think of the red bus.'

Instead, I have to actively *shift* my thoughts to something else, or pass my attention over to another thing.

There is a greatness to power shifting. When you pay too much attention to your anxiety, you suppress the person you *really want to be.*

Pay attention to how you want to feel rather than throw all your focus on how you *don't* want to feel. You can really start to move those mountains.

Activity

Attention feeds worry, so I want you to go to a place where your attention instead starves it.

You can do this with a focused and visualized meditation. This is a training process, so if you don't feel much the first time, that's okay. The key is trying.

Follow these steps to help get you started:

1. Find yourself in a position that sees you comfortable.

2. Set a timer. Be realistic, and go for something achievable at first, ten minutes.

3. Close your eyes, and fall into a consistent rhythm of breath. Focus on that alone as your mind wanders. Allow it. Wherever it wants to go, don't judge it, just let your thoughts pass like clouds.

Once your timer ends, spend the next few minutes in this clear, calm state of mind, perfectly visualizing the person you want to be.

Imagine yourself full of confidence, full of calm, and totally relaxed in different scenarios and situations. Imagine you. What do you see and hear? How do you feel being so calm? Get to know that person as you slowly morph into her.

Fixed Mindset

Thinking you can never change the way your mind thinks is one of the most common misconceptions about anxiety and negative thinking.

I like to think of the mind as a series of rivers and streams. Some are smaller than others, and some have very strong currents that pull the water (thoughts) along one way. The stronger the river, the harder the brain worked to build it.

If you imagine that every time you had a negative thought about something, it added more power to that river, and it flowed even harder than ever. That's because each thought is like a rock being put in place to manipulate the direction and flow of the river in your mind. That leaves me to ask you one *very important* question:

If you can create the flow of the river, you can create a change of direction.

In other words, those rocks can be picked up, and over time placed in other places that *change* or *alter* the river flow.

It *is* possible for your thoughts to change.

A fixed mindset is extremely trapping, especially with people who have anxiety.

Fixed mindsets lead to the belief that:

- **Change isn't possible**

- **Limitations keep you safe**

- **Opinions can't change**

- **Taking risks is dangerous**

- **It stops you from developing**

If you believe the roof above your head is your limit, rather than the sky, then you are stopping yourself from living the life you were destined for, because you are caught up in your mind. You believe it can't change, but I'm here to not only tell you, but confirm that it can.

Going from looking at your mindset, to changing it, is very possible, in fact, not only is it very possible, it is also very *likely* if you maintain the belief that you *can*. There are constant, small ways you can do this

Negative thoughts like to keep us in one place, but if you have anxiety, that one place is going to be far from ideal. There are so many ways to achieve growth within your mind, and the next chapter is going to really help you get started.

Chapter

4

LEARNING NEW THOUGHT PATTERNS

The *growth mindset* is key in anxiety recovery – and it is more than possible to achieve. American University professors Schleider, Abel, and Weisz conducted detailed studies with over 6500 students. Their findings revealed that those with a fixed mindset were 58% more likely to be showing symptoms of anxiety, stress, aggression and depression. More than that, in their research, they found those with fixed mindsets didn't believe they were able to improve their academic ability – leading to a decrease in self-esteem.

> "Believe you can, and you're halfway there."
> **- Theodore Roosevelt**

The growth mindset comes from looking at your current mind's 'roadmap,' and realizing that it doesn't exist even in the slightest way you'd hoped. All those little paths the mind is made to create are not reaching destinations that bring you calm and peace, and so something has to change.

The mindset, or how you think, is just like those rivers and streams I mentioned. How you change it, develops over time, but the fact that it *does* change, is key to overcoming all the anxiety you are carrying.

At the center of anxiety lies control, and if it is when people feel they *don't* have any the ,struggle really can begin.

I'm here to remind you that the belief that you cannot change your mindset is a fixed belief in itself - and that you're wrong - *so much can change for you.*

To change an unhelpful thought pattern, you must first recognize that it's there - that it exists. For that reason, there is a great level of self-reflection involved in learning new thought patterns.

Questioning your current thought patterns will help you understand them more. Remember - just because you have been used to this way of thought, doesn't mean you are even slightly aware of how they came about, or where or when you think of them. It's all natural to you right now, and not challenging them will allow them to continue freely.

Opening your eyes to your thought patterns will allow them to start shifting and changing in real time. This is where the magic truly begins, and where your anxiety levels can decrease.

Focus on What You Can Control

Feeling stressed about all those things you lack control of is normal, but why let it consume so much energy, when you *know* you can't change them? Easier said than done, I know. If you find the worry about the things out of your hands to be daily, and causes real changes to your day, then you know you have to take a little action.

Gaining a sense of control leads to a decrease in anxiety. If your anxiety is that you'll lose your job and end up with no money, are there ways you can put a little away each month to give you some savings that will ease this worry? If your worries can decrease with you making a few changes, and finding new ways to increase healthy habits - then start today.

It is possible to create distance between your thoughts and reality, and that is in how you perceive those thoughts. Looking at them as though they are in control will automatically give them that very power, and that will be something you are looking to avoid if you want to overcome your anxiety.

The power you give something will be the fuel that keeps it alive.

Two things you can start to look at are based around the concept of Cognitive Behavioral Therapy (CBT). CBT is a form of therapy that challenges the way we think and feel and how we respond to what happens to us. It allows us the space to understand that there are other ways of looking at things, therefore other ways of dealing with them.

1. **Thinking about all the things you *can* control**

Whether you believe it or not, you are in control of many things, starting with what you think and how you respond to those thoughts. Two concepts can change the entire way you deal with negative thoughts. To sit and think about this can pave the way for you to start opening doors in your mind that lead you to a place of positivity. More about what you can control can be found in chapter four.

2. **Writing down your thoughts**

Writing down your thoughts helps give you distance from them, because they come out of your mind and onto paper. That distance can sometimes be the rationality you need in order to realize how unhelpful they are.

The Stories of Real Women

Rose, 27

"My anxiety got to the point where I felt like everything was out of my control, even the small things I actually was able to get hold of and actually do something about. It's really strange, because the more my anxiety worsened, the less I believed I was able to change it, or fix it. It's a really trapping feeling, believing that this is my destiny for the rest of my life, but it wasn't. I did a lot of work on my mindset and

started to see that I was able to take control way more than I thought I could. It was life changing for me."

Elsie 38

I spent pretty much all of my twenties seeing my friends grow and get amazing jobs, and I constantly felt held back by the belief that I wasn't good enough to achieve the way they were. The more I stood still and watched them live their lives, graduating from uni, traveling, and eventually finding great jobs, the further behind I felt I was falling. It signaled huge failure to me, but it all stemmed from the simple thought that I wasn't clever enough to do what they were doing. Now I'm heading to 40, I've got my own business, and it's doing really well. It took time and effort to get here, it isn't as if someone waved a magic wand, but you have to want to challenge your anxiety, and you have to chase the freedom that comes with it."

Activity

A great way to start being aware of what you *can* control is to reframe how you think about them.

For example, a negative thought might be…

"I'm useless at being organized."

Your activity is to change that thought into something more positive and useful, such as:

"I can sometimes struggle with prioritization, but I am going to start making a small list each evening for what I need to do the next day."

Do you see how you can take something negative you feel about yourself and completely transform it?

Activity

Reframing is a way of giving the unhelpful stories you tell yourself a more positive spin.Practicing this will help relieve you of the burden your mind is holding from all the incorrect pieces of information your anxiety created that it believes to be true.

I want you to take one thing you believe that you know to be unhelpful. Is it how you feel about yourself or your career? Maybe it's the belief that you'll never find love.

Sit with that belief, and soon, you will feel those familiar, unhelpful thoughts arise, and from those thoughts will come emotions. That's how the brain works. It gives you a thought, and you respond emotionally to it.

When you reach the point where your unhelpful belief has brought about the responding emotions, ask yourself if those emotions are helpful to you. Be consciously aware that you are asking yourself, and you can do that by visualizing a version of yourself stepping back and looking at you from the outside.

Do Not Make Assumptions

If you were to get a text from your partner or a friend that seemed short, you're likely to think, 'what have I done wrong?' before you even contemplate, 'maybe I caught them at a busy time.' These kinds of thoughts are habitual, and ingrained into the anxious mind, but the assumption can be far from what is happening, or what is actually true. Jumping to conclusions is easier than knowing the truth, but there are ways you can clarify what's happening, and all involve ignoring those thoughts in your mind. Asking questions is a great place to start, or advice from a trusted and reliable person will give you the reassurance you need. Observing what's going on, rather than what you *think* will help you gauge the reality, rather than the worry behind your thoughts.

The Stories of Real Women

Emma, 44

"I used to assume the worst a lot of the time. I almost fell out with a friend a few years ago because I assumed her short texts were because I had" said or done something wrong. She was going through some financial difficulties and was embarrassed to speak up about it. We were able to talk about it but more so, I was able to reflect on how I handled the silence, and looking at how far from the truth my assumptions that I was at fault were to blame."

Ava, 25

"When I used to make assumptions, I was quick to go to the worst case scenario eery single time. I got to a point where I imagined situations like I was watching a film! It sounds crazy, but stepping back and observing meant I could see what was going on, rather than what I imagined. I started doing this because a small part of me knew I could be wrong about what I was assuming to be true. I'm glad I did, because hey, I was wrong, and now I can see that. There's real danger in assuming, and even more danger in believing what you assume."

Remove Your Mental Filters

Mental filters where you believe the stories you tell yourself to be totally true *can* be removed. Whilst nobody can remove them for you, there are a plethora of ways you can do this yourself, with a little time, love and patience.

Wrong conclusions lead to mental filters, where we only believe what we tell ourselves. If you think about it, how often do stories that you tell yourself lead to feeling overwhelmed with stress?

It can stop!

Putting your foot on the brake pedal and stepping outside your thoughts is a great initial way to speed up the process of removing your mental filters.

How can you do this? There are several ways.

1. Be positive to yourself

All the good things that are going on in your life can resort to the bottom of the pile when you approach it with anxiety. It's hard to see few positives when your mind is telling you so many other terrible things are going on that need your immediate attention, but if they are based on the stories you tell yourself, then they shouldn't really be given the room to grow. Be positive with yourself, and pick out all the good parts of your day.

2. Factor Fiction?

Be direct with yourself in times like this. To eradicate your mental filters, it's really helpful to ask yourself if what you are believing to be true is based on fact or fiction. This is crucial – it is a question that offers a direct answer, which can lead to solving the issue of your mental discomfort.

You are going to be late for work. You're going to be fired. Fact or fiction?

You won't sleep tonight because you have had such a stressful day. Fact or fiction?

If you start working with the rational part of your brain, you will understand how much it is there to help you.

3. Breathe deeply

Breathing deeply never fails to help reset your mind. It can be a few deep breaths to give you the mental pause you need, or you can take a few minutes to gain clarity and composure. Whatever you decide to do with your breathing, make sure you spend the time reconnecting with that fact or fiction thought, and use it to your advantage.

The Stories of Real Women

Izzy, 30

"I have this crazy 'tunnel vision' style thinking system that has got me into all kinds of trouble in the past. In fact, it was really the catalyst for my anxiety, and I didn't even really connect it until it was too late. Anxiety basically allows your thoughts to become facts. It doesn't stop until you truly believe what you're thinking, and it doesn't allow any room for change. Of course, the rational mind would disagree, and that's what you have to tap into in order to overcome the anxious thoughts and symptoms."

Fern, 42

"I suffered so much with my negative thoughts and found it stemmed from the way I used the internet. I used to go onto news outlets just to seek out the bad or worrying news. Price hikes. Rising costs of bills and mortgages. I got myself into a situation where I thought the world was crashing down around me, and I had no idea how I would keep the house warm or pay for everything. In looking for the bad stuff, I wasn't even giving all the good things any of my attention. There was a lot to

learn from the habits I had got myself into, and certainly a lot to un-learn!"

Activity

The stories you read are from real women who realized and overcame their own mental filters.

One way of beginning to overcome them is to see them for what they are - untrue and unhelpful.

Keeping a thought record will be the black-and-white imagery you need to help you see where and when your thoughts arise.

All you need to do is be aware of your negative thoughts. Be aware when you have one. Where are you? What were you doing right before the thought occurred?

When your negative thought starts to gain traction, be there with it and be the 'stop' sign.

Essentially, you are capturing your emotions that unravel from the negative thought, and diverting them away from you.

It's a small thing, but the more you practice it, the more aware you will become.

Letting Go

I want to start this section with one of my favorite quotes:

> "You'll never change your life until you change something you do daily. The secret of your success is found in your daily routine."
> **- John C. Maxwell.**

Negative thought patterns can become so deeply ingrained that you don't even know they're there.

When it comes to letting these patterns go, you might find yourself trying a few different ways before you find one that is successful.

Old habits die hard, but they are still there because they serve a purpose at some point in your life, even if it is to protect you or make you feel safe.

Accepting the habit that served you once upon a time but is now having a detrimental effect on you is something that takes real courage because it's like shedding a comfortable blanket that you have relied on for warmth over the years.

Knowing you need to change a thought pattern will automatically be something your mind tries to deflect. 'No! I don't think that's a good idea!' is pretty much how it will respond, and that is why it can take weeks for a new thought pattern or habit to form.

The attachment you have to an old thought is the fear of letting go - but when you *do* finally let go, you will notice the world opening up for you. One thought that is possible suddenly becomes a world of opportunity for a brand new - anxiety free - you.

Staying in your fear of letting go is only going to create more anxiety. As you try to push down the walls and fight for your freedom, you'll only end up grappling with yourself and losing momentum on any progress you've made so far.

Letting go is that moment where you dip your toes is like being on an island in an ocean full of change, and everybody is calling you to dive in and enjoy it. Releasing what has been trapping you is life-changing, but only you can do it.

The Stories of Real Women

Catherine, 28

"Letting go of my anxiety was like letting go of an attachment. It was so strange - I learned to live with it, and learned to 'cope,' even though I knew my anxiety levels were far from healthy. I kept my comfort zone small and avoided anything that heightened my worry and racing thoughts. Soon enough, that wasn't enough, and I worried about every little thing. I tried so hard not to be anxious, but all that did was make me more worried and frustrated. Letting go wasn't easy. It was like letting go of everything I used to keep myself safe when, in fact, I wasn't safe; I was cocooned. Now, I still get anxious, but my mind has learned new patterns to get me out of the rut I was stuck in for so many years. One of the key things I do every day is avoid the news. If I hear it, I hear it, but I don't go out of my way to source negativity, because then I can focus on myself more."

Lou, 35

"Letting go was simply not an option for me. I had no idea I had so much to let go of though, and assumed (incorrectly) that I had it all under control. It was clear I didn't when I had a panic attack in the London Underground last summer, and I knew then that something had to change. I was frantically worried about myself, and worry only breeds more worry. My negative thoughts were out of control, and so was my anxiety. Therapy helped, but implementing the changes I needed made the real difference. It started small, but I reframed my thoughts one by one. There's no time to stumble or stop, because you won't get anywhere, but my mindset became freer and freer by the week, and now I am able to detach myself from those apocalyptic thoughts that don't serve me at all."

Jan, 45

"Letting go was my main challenge. I was constantly being told, just let go, and start to see the world differently." It wasn't that easy for me. Coming out of a failed marriage meant I had to form so many new thought patterns to help me overcome not only the loss, but the failure behind it that seemed to ignite my anxiety even more. Accepting that some things just don't work out was the most work, because with that came all the ways I tried to cope that led to an unhealthy me. I'm taking it step by step, but I am getting there."

Activity

Clearing your mind of the negative thought clutter that has kept it feeling chaotic and heavy all this time is tricky, but there are simple tools to help you.

One known way of clearing the mind, and being the cure for paying too much attention, is to separate yourself from what's plaguing you.

1. Sit comfortably, and prepare yourself with a few nice deep breaths.

2. Imagine you are amongst some dark, stormy clouds in the sky. Within those clouds are all your old thought patterns, negative and stagnant. Visualize those as any object you wish. They're spinning around you as if you are in a tornado.

3. Start slowly rising in your mind, away from the clouds. The objects, your thoughts, become smaller. The chaos starts to quieten. Your view of the clutter gets smaller, and smaller, until you feel a safe distance away from it.

4. Picture yourself now high up in the unchanging sky. It's gorgeous. It's serene. It's a deep, dark blue that you cannot compare to anything else.

5. Now listen to your mind, as it offers nothing back but stillness.

6. Look down on your old thought patterns and see yourself detached from them.

This activity will help you initially see that you are not attached to your old thought patterns as much as you thought you were. In visualizing yourself apart, you can then form healthier ones.

Chapter

5

STOP OVERTHINKING

Rumination and overthinking are ways your anxiety tries to prepare for something that has yet to happen, and may never (the likelihood is never) happen). Overthinking is nearly always negative, but the brain does it to interfere with what you're doing at that time.

In fact, in 2005, the APA (American Psychological Association) Defined rumination as:

"Obsessional thinking involving excessive, repetitive thoughts or themes that interfere with other forms of mental activity."

Worrying more doesn't make your mind problem-solve any harder. You aren't going to gain some magical insight into your worries by allowing them to command a huge portion of your time. Worry only invites more worry.

You are able to stop this cycle and prevent yourself from

spiraling into more unhappiness and anxiety.

You don't have to be perfect, and I understand that much overthinking comes from wanting to be so, as well as not wanting to fail. Failure by default will occur if you worry so much that you cannot achieve your goals anyway.

Overthinking and rumination are ways your brain will actively revert to worst-case scenarios that you can control, I repeat, *can control.*

Find a distraction

Distractions from rumination will work to decrease the levels you are overthinking and the effect they are having on your mental, emotional, and physical self. I need to stress something at this point, because distractions can come in all forms, and it's important you find what works for you. Having *said* that, you need to find distractions that are:

- **Healthy**

- **Helpful**

- **Encouraging**

- **Empowering**

If you find that canceling one negative habit with another is conducive to good health and wellbeing, then you are going to be in very temporary waters indeed. Examples of the kind of distraction I'm referring to, that would *not* help you are:

- **Smoking**

- **Drinking**

- **Gambling**

- **Emotional eating**

- **Over-exercising**

Any of the above might feel good in the moment, but all you're doing is replacing one problem with another.

The distractions you need should be more about how you want to grow and the direction you want your mind to travel. There is no room for more negativity in your life, and you deserve far more than simply obtaining another habit that will damage you in some way.

Exercising is a great way to distract yourself, but you have to stay healthy and not overdo it. Finding things that work is easy - there *has* to be something to suit you.

- **Dancing**

- **Joining a club**

- **A hobby that involves 'doing' such as knitting, sewing, decoupage, drawing or writing**

- **Running**

- **Walking**

- **Birdwatching**

- **Litter picking for your community**

- **Volunteering at an animal shelter or school**

- **Reading**

- **Watching your favorite TV show**

- **Meeting up with a friend**

- **Calling a friend or family member for a catch-up**

- **Good old housework!**

- **Making a nice soup or salad for lunch from scratch**

Some of these things take five minutes, others can take hours. It depends on what you want to do and how often you want to do it in order to set yourself a new routine that allows less time for rumination.

Stories

"The worst part of my anxiety, when it was at its most uncontrollable, was overthinking. I used to love my own company, and I didn't realize that being alone meant I had the time to sit and contemplate every possible outcome. Those outcomes were never good. I convinced myself once that my husband was going to leave me because he was frequently late home from work. It was only when he showed me his route home on his Maps app that I saw the amount of roadworks he had to endure daily. It was then I knew I had to distract myself whenever I started overthinking, and now I enjoy my time in the garden or call a friend if I feel it creeping on. Overthinking is a trap!"

- Jenny, 31

"Distractions were the last thing I thought I needed when I started to ruminate. Never did I imagine myself thinking, "Right, I need to do something before I go totally mad!" - but I had to. Distractions are like interruptions in my mind. I don't have the energy to create stories in my head any more, especially not with three kids all under the age of five!" - Cassie - 39

Activity

The next time you feel yourself overthinking, I want you to get up immediately. Don't give yourself time to question getting up, find yourself on your feet.

1. Head to the nearest place you can play music, whether through a device, your phone or laptop.

2. Turn on the one song guaranteed to get you dancing. It doesn't matter how cheesy it is, in fact, the cheesier the better!

3. Dance. Dance as if nobody's watching.

4. It'll be a good 3 to 3 and a half minutes until you finish. When you do and you stop, out of breath most likely, how do you feel now?

5. Notice the blood pumping around your body, your heart beating fast, your lungs breathing in air quickly.

6. Be consciously grateful that those symptoms are from a fun dance, rather than your anxiety from overthinking.

Make a plan

Making that shift from ruminating to problem-solving is going to go against the waves of anxiety you currently experience. It's going to be a little like trying to swim to the shore from the sea, but that doesn't mean it's at all impossible.

Your mind has become firmly lodged in the, 'I do what I can to survive' way of thinking - which is that overthinking part of you you're losing yourself too at the moment, but you don't have to submit to it, and you don't have to commit to it either.

Making a plan to problem-solve your way out of rumination is a process that will *actively* ask you to take part. You'll want to try, but your mind will do its best to do what it does best - keep you where you are.

The way to escape overthought is to break it down and ask yourself to find solutions. For example, if you are worrying about meeting a work deadline, you might break your worry down into small steps so that you can set aside time to complete what you need to do.

If you are overly anxious about paying a bill on time, you can put aside money each month to ensure that doesn't happen again. Even if it means you give up a few coffees to go, you can instead put it into a savings account that means you don't have to worry about where the sudden chunk of money to pay that bill will come from.

If you are prone to feeling insecure in your relationship, being concerned about whether or not your partner is cheating will come from somewhere in your mind. When did you start thinking this way? What else is going on with you? What evidence do you actually have? What is going on with your partner right now, and are they going through tough times themselves to make them feel or seem distant? Redirecting your energy can save you time, pain, and the possibility of a relationship ending based on your thoughts alone.

Make a plan to find out these answers rather than the answers your mind has created. I understand. When you think and overthink, what you're overthinking can seem so *real*. Your brain thinks they are, and that is why you respond to the thoughts with such anxiety.

Being empowered to stop rumination in its tracks and tackle it head on is something you are all capable of feeling. You deserve it too, because overthinking can be exhausting. Day or night, it's enough to make you want to scream, but you *can* quieten the thoughts down, and you *can* achieve mind serenity.

Make a deal with yourself to start challenging your thoughts, and to look at them as math problems, rather than real issues you have to deal with. The problem arises when anxiety actually turns your rumination into reality simply by thinking of them in real life. If you're worried you can't sleep, you'll be unlikely to be able to. That's not you being *right*, that is your anxiety about it keeping you awake.

Stories

"Honestly, the best thing you can do for yourself is come up with some

plan to help you get out of those sticky overthinking episodes. They really are like being sucked into a black hole. I'll always have anxious tendencies, but I am fully aware that my overthinking habits have got me into a lot of trouble before. I have had confrontations with everyone from people I work with, to my kids' teachers, because I overthought small issues to the point where I'd snowballed them into unmanageable sizes. Why? Simply because I mistook my anxiety for something that was trying to protect me, but in fact, it was harming me." - Emma, 34

"Plans are good, and you will work far better with one because you will always have something to go to if you feel lost. A plan is a little bit like customer service tills as a kid when you're at the supermarket. If you feel lost, head there and you can be reunited with your parents again, or in this case, your sanity and rational thinking! That's how I like to see it anyway." - Jude, 44

Activity

When rumination hits you, you need a plan.

When a thought crops up, write it down. Don't hesitate, write.

1. Be specific with what you're writing. Be honest. What is it bothering you?

2. How can you challenge it? What's your plan? Do you want to do something practical to help ease the worry, or is it totally irrational and something you need to erase?

3. Think about how you can solve it, and if it is a real problem, or simply something you're worrying about that hasn't or isn't happening?

4. When you gain information, start addressing the issue, step by step.

Disrupting your rumination with a plan will help it crumble before you so that it no longer exists.

Make a decision

Overthinking decisions will lead to clearer views of what it is you are trying to decide on. You'll go back and forth, should I ? Shouldn't I? You'll weigh up the options, the what ifs, the consequences - the 'everything.'

It's very healthy to think, and to contemplate, but if you go too deeply, you will talk yourself out of things, and refuse to budge based on the fact that your mind has created a thousand and one scenarios, none of which have even begun to come true.

Overthinking will prevent you from taking action, and sometimes that in itself can be the cycle you actually quite like. It's that you *don't* like making choices, so overthinking keeps you in a comfortable place of limbo.

Not deciding what to do will keep you from committing to things, things that may seem scary to you because you want them, or don't want them so much. Ask yourself, though - is it truly better to stay in the land of nothing? Is it really helpful to avoid decision-making altogether?

Making that conscious choice to stop overthinking is going to be your catalyst for how you treat the rest of your anxiety. Imagine, for a moment, a life of peace. Where you can go to bed at night and sleep soundly knowing that all those thoughts once circling have now been put to rest.

It's harder than it seems to get into the habit, but the decision to start fixing your overthinking to more stable, helpful thoughts is going to be what gives you peace of mind, and what gets you out of them ental torture of imagining such negative outcomes.

Ways you can strengthen your decision to stop overthinking are:

- Letting go of what perfection looks like in your mind. Perfection doesn't exist anywhere.

- Find that intuitive part of you that thinks, 'What if I thought *this* way, instead of *that?*

- Put your problems into some perspective. Actively encourage yourself to ask, 'Am I thinking about this too much?'

- Think about all the ways your life can improve if you just stepped away from your thoughts, and allowed them to die without your anxious energy keeping them alive.

- Empower yourself in the knowledge that your anxiety is a level of sensitivity that helps you connect with people, not overthink your way to disaster.

- Building your confidence by knowing that overthinking is a choice that evolves into an ingrained habit that you can erase.

- Conquer the fear that the worst is always right on your doorstep.

We are all alive, and we all need to make decisions. Some of them might prove difficult because we are scared of what comes next. Your brain will try to look after you, but your heart wants to lead you to places that make you feel happy. Which one do you go with when it comes to decisions? Of course, there's no reason to follow your goals if they are going to create detrimental outcomes, but if you truly want something, biting the bullet and seeing where your curiosity leads you is what life is all about.

I know that decisions come with any consequence, and you have to be realistic that not all things work out the way you want them to, but if you don't try, you'll never know.

Stories

"The day you decide to make a choice to alter the overthinking part of your mind is the day you make huge, huge changes. Believe me. I got so caught up in my head that I couldn't see a way out. It was awful. I couldn't help myself, every time I was on my own or had excess time, there I was, thinking the worst, assuming this would happen, wondering what the dreadful outcome would be if I did or didn't do something. All

I was doing was sitting down by myself on my couch, who knew it would be so damaging. I ended up hating that part about me that I couldn't bear to hold onto it any longer. Decide who you want to be, and what layers you want to shed - and go and do it as soon as you can." - Zoe - 40

"I plan for overthinking, but I try not to plan too much because I know life can happen and unexpected directions take you places you didn't expect. If I start overthinking, my plan of action is to move. It doesn't matter where I am, I get up and I start from there. If I'm at home, I tidy or put some music on. If I have the time, I'll bake something, or cook. I like to have a method before me, or instructions to follow so that I don't slip back into my chair and start overthinking again. The clock can feel stuck when you get into that habit, but if I do something, it starts moving again. It's either that or I imagine the worst, and convince myself that all my thoughts are true." - Lucie - 28

"I was so afraid of leaving my comfort zone. I was at a point in my life where I could physically see and feel everything changing. I outgrew many ideas, a few people, and ways of thinking because through therapy my anxiety had become something I could see from the outside, rather than feel on the inside. I was always told I am only one decision away from a totally different life, and those people were right. I was, and through deciding to leave my ex partner meant I could get to know myself. The way I overthink. My triggers. Everything. I was scared, but I was successful in looking at my thoughts and knowing there were far too many of them." - Vanessa, 36

Activity

Overthinking is always something you have the choice to do or ignore. Listening to your fears and worries will help them to grow.

1. Promise yourself every day that you are going to stop overthinking

2. Each morning when you wake, consciously think, even say, 'I am not going to overthink anything today. What will be, will be.'

3. When you feel yourself beginning to fall back during the day, take yourself right back to the morning and reaffirm your message to yourself.

This is a small activity with many benefits, because it is there to put you back on track whenever you feel derailed.

Reassess your goals

It is believed by many that overthinking kills willpower. Think about it. You wake up after the promise of going for a run every morning. It is now morning and you are laying in bed. You think about the weather, and peek out the window. It looks dark, possibly cold even. You start to mentally scan your body and notice a few aches. You aren't really awake yet, and it's not a good idea to just jump out of bed and go exercise. The more you think about it, the more you think your throat feels scratchy. You worry, because you have important things to finish at work, and you can't afford to be off sick. You worry even more because you want to work on getting fitter and being healthier, and you can't do that if you are sick or achy. Why do you ache, anyway?

Do you see? One goal, completely diminished by your anxious overthinking, creating excuses that lead to fear and worry, and more anxiety.

'Goals' is such a big word to people with anxiety. It normally attaches itself to pressure, or time, or fear. The main assumption is, 'what could go wrong?' rather than, 'what could go right?' What if you succeed? What if you smash your goals and develop and grow, and laugh and live, and know what it feels like to work toward something successfully without being distracted by too many thoughts?

Stories

"I know that when I overthink, I need new goals. It's like I 've got to the bottom of the glass of water, and there are only a few drops left, and I need to refill it. When my brain gets stuck, seriously stuck in thought, it's likely because I don't have direction. Having that focus helps pull me out of the rut I'm stuck in. Honestly - it's the worst. The only good thing about it all is that I am aware, and that's only because I studied my anxiety in detail, and I got to know myself well enough to spot the signs." - Lily, 32

"Life gets to the point where you need to look at your goals and make sure you are working towards them. If you aren't, why not? You can either make progress, or make excuses in my eyes, and I always like to

know I am taking steps towards mine. It helps distract me from ruminating. I know my thoughts occur because I want to try and control every aspect of life, but in doing that, I am pulled away from my goals, of which I am in full control of! It's funny really how anxiety thinks it's doing you a favor, when in fact all it does is hold you back." - Sally, 26

Activity

Goals work best when you hold yourself accountable for them.

1. If you have a goal in mind, work through it in writing in detail. What do you want?

2. Write down how you want to get it. Ways in which you can help yourself.

3. Where will you be?

4. How long will it take?

5. Can you achieve it in steps?

6. What might derail you - always be prepared and aware of your weaknesses.

7. Use a calendar to mark days you can check in with your goal, and watch your progress.

8. Make a point to reassess your goal every Monday (or whatever day works for you).

These bitesize ways to get you from A to B will give you the time you need to get what you want without falling or slipping behind.

Chapter

6

LIFESTYLE IMPROVEMENT FOR LONG-TERM WELL BEING

If you think it isn't possible to improve your circumstances, you're wrong. Many people with anxiety choose to continue to live the life they know well, even if they don't like it, because it is familiar, and they see no other way to be. This is a frequent mistake made, and it's usually accompanied by coping mechanisms or avoidance tactics that allow the anxiety to lay dormant, but not eradicated.

Covering up anxiety is a dangerous thing because there's no telling when it will erupt like a volcano. You could be anywhere, any time, and a panic attack could hit because you have swept your challenges under the carpet instead of looking at them and understanding that you can improve them by improving *yourself*.

I don't want that for you, and you shouldn't want it for yourself either. The simple and sole reason being:

You have it within your power every single day to improve your lifestyle for long-term well-being.

If it sounds hard to believe, it's because you've never fully taken the time to explore all the possible ways your well-being can improve with steps towards a healthier mind, with healthier habits. Being kind to yourself is the only way you can open the doors to more opportunity for self-care, better sleep, and to inject all-important positivity into your days, rather than continue to allow them to be filled with thoughts that don't help you, and that keep you suppressed from a life of true contentment.

Is that something you can start working on this very day?

Lifestyle change is essential to reduce your anxiety symptoms.

Sleep - Sleep is the foundation for which everything else sits upon. Without rest, for both body and mind - you cannot think straight. This only leads to already poor decision-making moments to worsen rather than improve, and ultimately leads to a poor contribution to your already existing anxiety.

Relaxation - Finding ways to relax is *crucial.* If you can't relax, you will end up living in a constant state of fear, worry and anticipation. If your mind and body is relaxed, those symptoms of anxiety won't be able to take over, and make you feel the way they do.

Self-care - You're worth looking after, and nobody else is really going to do it for you the way you can do it for yourself. It is far more than just running a bath or listening to soothing music (although those things *do* help), and it is a huge way of improving your well-being.

Exercise - Exercise is movement, and movement releases all the anxious tension in your body that builds up through worry, overthinking, catastrophizing and assuming the worst. It fights the negative, stress hormones and replaces them with the good ones.

Positive self-talk - Every positive outcome starts with a positive input. Inputting that information into your mind on a conscious level is tricky when all you've done is tell it not so great things, but when you learn how, you unroll the carpet of positivity that leads you to a better life. It's time you walked that carpet.

Knowing all these things can help improve your well-being is one thing, but *implementing* them is quite another. Luckily, you are now at a point where you can start doing some really life-changing activities and meditations to help you, and that is where this chapter can help you.

Sleep well

Anxiety is well connected to sleep problems. Worries and fears become trapped in our minds to the point where they cannot escape, even at bedtime. This makes it harder to either fall asleep, or stay asleep, or both. The problem begins with sleep deprivation, worsening the symptoms of anxiety. It is well known that mental health issues seem so much more magnified when we are tired. Our brains haven't had the rest they need. You're tired, and cloudy minded - and that's how a cycle of *insomnia* can begin and be extremely difficult to break.

Now is the time to start understanding the link between not sleeping and your own anxiety.

Tips For A Good Night's Sleep

- **Try to maintain a consistent routine**

From the moment we are born, we thrive with nighttime routines. These go out the window the older we get, when we start heading out, staying up late to watch TV, or working shift patterns. The body has a programme that likes to know when it's going to go to bed, and there are things you can do to prepare it for that. Keeping a nightly routine, where bedtime (and waking up time) is roughly the same, helps keep you on a track that allows for a pattern to develop, leading to consistent sleep.

- **Night time tea helps**

Any tea with chamomile, lavender, ashwagandha, or valerian root will all help you relax and feel at ease with your day. Always check with your doctor that these teas are okay to consume, depending on your health conditions or possible medication that you're on.

- **Turn off the screens**

Smartphones, computers, laptops, TV - make sure you go an hour without screens before you lay your head down. The light of the screens emit a blue light, making it hard to switch your mind off. Keeping it active and awake isn't what you want before you attempt to sleep. It also suppresses a hormone called melatonin, which is your body's natural sleep aid. Without it, sleep will be incredibly difficult.

- **Write down your worries before bed**

Putting your worries onto paper helps release them from your mind. If they're out of your mind, they can lessen the chaos you take to bed with you. This will help promote a clear sleep without being bugged or plagued by mind matters. It can also help you detach from your worries, and teach you that you can observe them on paper, instead of constantly feeling them within.

- **Don't obsess over sleep, or lack of it**

Spending your days looking at your bed as if it is the enemy is going to set you up for a fall as soon as the lights go out. Your bed isn't your enemy, it's your safe haven, your place to rest. Make friends with it, and if you are struggling to fall asleep, tell yourself that it's okay and that it doesn't matter. Giving your worry power will keep the worry alive longer.

- **Exercise during the day**

Quash those stress hormones with happier ones by promoting an exercise regime. You can do whatever works for you, as long as it's physical. Keep to exercising during the day or early evening, and avoid it up to two hours before bed so you can truly wind down and allow yourself the sleep you deserve.

- **Try not to nap during the day**

Napping during the day not only disturbs your sleep pattern, but it allows you the time to snooze off your fatigue before it's actually time to commit those several hours of quality shut eye. I know how hard it is to not nap, but staying awake will be how you become fully ready for bedtime - *at* bedtime.

- **Keep cool and check your environment**

It's known that having a bedroom that's too warm will keep you awake as you shift and move to find cool spots. Be calm, be cool, be comfortable with a room between 16 and 18°C for optimum sleep. Equally, keep your room free of clutter and calm in color to create a really relaxed ambience.

- **Keep it dark**

Darkness is what your brain needs to know it is bedtime, without the distraction of light. In the summer, invest in blackout blinds to keep that darkness in check.

Activity

It's bedtime, and you want to get a full night's rest, only this is something you continuously struggle with.

1. A few hours before you go to bed, crack open your bedroom

window (making sure you keep any children or animals away from it).

2. Ensure your bed is made nicely, ready for you to enter it.

3. If there is any clutter you can move with ease and store somewhere, try to do it, or at least make your side of the bed clear.

4. Pop on a lamp, and shut the door.

5. In the time before you head to bed, pick out your favorite book, or something you've got and been meaning to read, and try to read a chapter (or a few pages, depending on what you can manage).

6. If you aren't a reader, pop on a nice, relaxing podcast to listen to.

7. When it comes to bedtime, enter your bedroom and try to absorb the wonderful atmosphere you created.

Little routines like this, or promises to yourself to have a welcoming bedtime will help you see that you are in control of what you create, and where you spend your time.

Meditation Activity

Pre-bed is a great time to meditate, so try to find somewhere cozy to clear your mind before you head upstairs. If it helps, set a timer for a duration that suits you and is realistic. 15 minutes is often good to start with, but you can work your way up to more.

1. Once you get yourself comfortable, I want you to allow all your thoughts to come and go. Visualize your ears as entry and exit points for everything you think. Allow them in, allow them out, without thought, frustration or judgment.

2. Breathe in, breathe out. Keep a calm, steady rhythm.

3. Use your meditation time to fully unwind and be in the moment.

4. If you find your mind wandering, let it. Just be the observer of your thoughts by noticing them and allowing them to go again.

This practice will help you see your thoughts, but not *be* them. It's all about control.

Relaxation

I have lost count of the amount of women who tell me they are told those four magic words frequently.

Try not to worry.

I wonder if you have been told those words before, from people who mean well and have good intentions. Their concern for your anxiety goes no further than a simple comment of advice that they honestly feel will bring some comfort to you. Unfortunately, those who suffer and have to live each day with anxiety are not going to be cured by *trying not to worry.* It goes beyond that.

'Try not to worry' doesn't bring about a wave of relaxation, but there *is* something to take from it certainly, in the 'try' part.

It *does* take effort to stop worrying, and you *do* have to try (although not too hard - otherwise you'll end up more frustrated than you were to begin with). To try is to be consciously aware that you need an energy shift in order to gain control of the mental distress caused by your anxiety. That energy shift is the effort it takes to get from A to B, or 'worry' to 'calm.' Once you reach calm, you will be able to relax a lot easier.

Relaxation is like a friend that's always there for you, but you forget they're there. It's always an option to choose relaxation, but sometimes, if you're anxiety inclined, it's hard to channel the part of your brain that promotes relaxation. It's almost as if the door to entry is firmly shut, and the more you think you want to open it, the harder it becomes. However - you have the key to that door at all times in your very hand, and if you frame your thoughts positively enough, turning it in the lock is absolutely possible.

The purpose of relaxation for *anybody* is to slow the heart rate and begin to manage your physical, mental and physiological symptoms that stress or anxiety brings. Those with long term worry and anxiety will feel in a constant state of stress to some level, brought on by the anxiety that fuels their thoughts, so it's important to find techniques that suit you, so that you can relax every day.

Relaxation techniques are also very handy for pulling you away from your worries, because to have distance from them allows you to have a more rational perspective.

Remember - your aim through this book is to find out more about yourself, why you feel the way you do, and how to do something about the anxiety you constantly live in a state of. Relaxation is a *process* that gives your mind and body the peace it needs. Even better, relaxation techniques are all free or low cost, and you can do them anywhere. This leaves little excuse to start making improvements to your life right now.

Benefits of relaxation techniques

If you live your anxious life constantly tense, with your body constantly feeling as though a threat is right around the corner, any kind of relaxation to lessen that is going to be exactly what you need. More and more people are becoming hardwired to react every day to something that promotes anxiety symptoms. Anxiety is prevalent in society, and most of those who experience it accept it, and run on stress and adrenaline, but it just isn't healthy. What your aim should be is to exchange the weight on the scales, so the tipping point becomes in your favor, rather than in favor of your anxiety.

In case you weren't already sold on the idea of providing each day with one or more relaxation techniques, here are some benefits to doing so:

- **Slower your heart rate**

- **Lower your blood pressure**

- **Eradicate or lessen your anger**

- **Lower stress levels**

- **Control your blood sugar levels**

- **Lessen or eradicate fatigue**

- **Boost your confidence**

- **Help you problem solve**

- **Regulates your stress hormone response**

- **Increases blood flow to muscle groups, which in turn eases tension and pain**

- **Slow down your breathing rate**

Autogenic relaxation

This type of relaxation comes from within and is all about using imagery to help calm you. You can focus on your breathing, and slow your heart rate down by being aware of your body, and paying attention to it as you relax. It is about being with yourself.

Progressive muscle relaxation

This is popular for people trying to fall asleep. This is about tensing and relaxing your muscles in different parts of your body. It brings awareness to yourself, and helps you determine when you are feeling tense, and realize those moments you're relaxing.

Visualization

Popular for many, visualization involves picturing yourself somewhere that makes you calm, and bringing it to life in your head. Sights, sounds, smells can help bring it to life, taking you to a palace of comfort.

Other popular ways to relax include:

- **Tai chi**

- **Walking**

- **Aromatherapy**

- **Yoga**

- **Massage**

- **Meditation**

- **Music or art therapy**

Activity

If you're having trouble with relaxation, think about the visualization aspect of it you just read about.

Do you have a favorite place you love to go or somewhere you imagine to make you very calm?

It is to float in the shallow shoes of aqua, calm seawater.

Close your eyes and take a few deep breaths, allowing your mind and heart to realize there is no current threat.

Think about yourself in your favorite place. Where is it? Is the sky blue? What can you smell and see? How do you feel? Is the sun warm on your skin?

Maybe it's somewhere cozy, like a log cabin in the middle of a forest, and you're watching the snow silently fall.

Give yourself ten minutes to get lost in the visualization, and relax into it. Doing this regularly will do wonders when it comes to relaxation.

Self-care activities

Many people mistake self-care for grabbing a nice bubble bath, and for many, that does the job. It feels great, and you get to wind down whilst warming your muscles up.

If you regularly become filled with anxiety, it's likely that a bubble bath every now and then isn't going to cut it for you, and that's where self-care goes to the next level.

A Vagaro Survey study saw 64% of people who prioritized their self-care felt a confidence boost after doing something for themselves, and a whopping 71% saw an increase in happiness. Imagine putting yourself first on a daily basis - the results would be even higher!

The aspects of self-care vary for those who seek it. Some see it as movement, whilst others see it as journaling. There is no right or wrong way to look after yourself, so long as what you do doesn't have a detrimental effect on you or anybody else.

Applying a little self-care in your life takes one single, initial thought:

I must start putting myself first - before anything - including my anxiety.

Knowing this is the platform you need as your starting point.

The list of ways to help you relax in section 6.2 is a list of things you can do to care for yourself. It isn't exclusive, but the aim is to make small lifestyle changes that help manage your anxiety symptoms. Regular self-care may also prevent your symptoms from getting worse or developing further.

You can maintain your wellbeing by putting self-care at the top of your list of priorities.

- **Spot early warning signs**

You delved into what triggers are earlier on in the book, and this knowledge will help you look at yourself and realize what your own early warning anxiety signs are. Being aware of how you're feeling and spotting when you start to feel unwell or overwhelmed can help you either reach out for support or give yourself the support you need. Remember - reaching out for support is still a form of self-care.

- **Work on your social life**

You don't have to be the center of attention or at every party. You certainly don't need copious amounts of friends in order to have a social life. However, if there is something you have always wanted to do, like join a book club, go to the movies more with a friend or relative, or even get out walking or swimming at your local pool - it should be something you actively think about applying into your day. Self-care is about giving your mind the boost it needs, and to make memories that nourish you, rather than fill you with dread. It's so important to feel connected to other people, whether that's one other, or ten others. If you don't feel ready for that, a simple text or phone call is a good starting point for getting the job done.

- **Make time for nature**

Nature is a known healer for anxious minds. There's something about the calm, green environment we live amongst that eases minds and worries, and makes for a great distraction.

- **Look after your physical self**

Sleep, physical activity, and eating right are all ways you can look after yourself physically. It's a form of self-care that will keep your body feeling well throughout all the anxious processes it experiences.

Other activities for self-care can be:

- **Ending your shower with a cold blast**

Cold water will give you a huge burst of energy as it gets your circulation going. It also releases endorphins - win-win!

- **Drink plenty of water**

Water is our very essence - we need lots of it every day. Keep yourself well hydrated, and you will notice the difference within hours.

- **Take a little walk on your lunch break if you can**

Some fresh air, a change of scenery, a little light exercise and a break from the people you work with. Perfect!

- **Make a deal to moisturize**

Moisturizing is often something we forget entirely to do, omitting the fact that our skin is an organ, and it needs taking care of. It's just a small thing - but it's for you.

- **Plan a getaway - even if it is virtual!**

More and more people head away for a few days to catch some self-care time, but with many people on budgets, there is a lot to be said for finding a place in the world, and heading to video search engines to find tours of cities/towns/beaches. You can sample the food by researching local culture, and try it out for yourself too. A proper staycation!

- **Join an online support group**

Online support groups must never be overrated they are priceless. See what you can find either on social media or via anxiety charities local to you.

Exercise

You'll know by now that exercise, as previously recommended in other sections, is a great way to reduce your anxiety. There is an element of struggling with many anxious sufferers who initially want to get into exercising, because the brain will come up with a dozen reasons why it isn't a good idea, or a plethora of excuses as to not do it. A recent study in Sweden found that in nearly 400,000 people, 60% of them were less likely to experience anxiety symptoms compared to those less active. You literally cut your chances of suffering with uncontrolled anxiety by over half if you exercise.

Do you remember the days of the COVID pandemic, where we were given a certain allocated amount of time to go outdoors and walk or exercise? I cannot count the number of people I knew who relied on that hour or so to be outside running or walking. It was a window of opportunity to release all the stress and worry that had naturally built up inside them. Now we are back to normality where we have much more time to consider exercising, it seems as though for many, it is out of reach.

There may be self-esteem issues, or worry surrounding overexertion. The time now is to put yourself first, because that is precisely what this entire chapter is about. Your wellbeing matters, which means your physical health also matters.

The aim of understanding and recognizing your anxiety is to intercept it as much as you can before it really starts to take hold. Know the warning signs, and instead of pushing past them, see them and work through them. You can do that with exercise because exercise is your body's way of responding to it helpfully. Think of all that energy anxiety produces. All those hormones prepare your body for the fight of your life when you aren't preparing at all for any violence. Instead, use that 'get ready' within you to exercise. Allow the energy to leave your body, otherwise it will hold onto it and make you feel even worse.

Why is exercise so important?

If you think you are too unfit for any time of exercise, I want you to find relief in the fact that scientists have actually found that exercising for just five minutes is enough to stimulate anti-anxiety symptoms or effects. If you are moving for those few minutes, the goodness your body receives is significant. Exercise also has been shown to improve sleeping patterns and self-esteem, as well as decrease tension and stress. Your mood in general is therefore stabilized - so really - exercise is like the pebble you throw that lands in the pool of water, and the positive repercussions for you, are the many, many ripples.

To function in a post-anxiety world, changes are essential. Applying an element of exercise into your day doesn't have to overwhelm you. If you start off each morning dancing to your favorite song, that's a great place to start. If you live near a park, adding a lap of that into a few days per week is also great.

The power of endorphins!

Endorphins are a hormone that trigger positive feelings in the body, and are released when people exercise. Accompanying endorphins is usually higher energy, which battles the feelings of anxiety and the worry behind your thoughts.

Exercise also:

- Strengthens your bones

- Lowers blood pressure

- Strengthens your heart

- Makes you *feel* good

Exercise is important, but so is picking the appropriate one for you. This means you're less likely to make excuses not to do it.

Exercise Activities

The first thing I would love for you to do is think about yourself. What do you like? If you had to pick an exercise to try, what would it be?

This isn't a long activity - but it is a crucial initial one to get you started.

1. Make a list of the different kinds of exercises you can think about - even if you can't see yourself trying them.

2. Once your list is complete, go through it and highlight the ones you like the sound of.

3. Working with this smaller list, think about the one you feel would be the most fun, the most suited to your schedule, and how long you could do the exercise for. It might be five minutes

- that's okay.

4. Try it!

Activity

Your aim from the previous activity is to see how you feel after you have exercised. Compare it to your mood before you started, and if there is a *slight* change, or you feel like you have exerted some of your anxious energy, why not try it again tomorrow?

Sit with your feelings post-exercise. Notice how differently you feel. Your heart is racing for a justified, good reason. Are you out of breath? Does your face feel warm? Does it feel good to have these feelings without anxiety being the culprit?

Positive self-talk / Positive affirmations

Why live in a world where all you do is talk negatively to yourself? It seems counterproductive to you, and everything you do when you do it all in response to this negative run of self-talk in your mind, so that's why it's best to attempt a more positive approach.

I'm fully aware of how difficult that can be, but you can promote change by thinking the change into place. Positive thoughts allow you to focus on positive behaviors.

They are also *very* helpful when it comes to panic attacks because you are counteracting the fear you are overcome with. Repetitive affirmations and self-talk that promotes a new way of thinking is going to see you reaching above your anxiety, and finding yourself calmer and happier.

Positive Affirmations to Try

Positive affirmations are the encouragement you need to start *believing* them.

- **I don't have to have it all worked out at this moment in time**

- **I am enough**

- **Perfection isn't something I strive to achieve**

- **My anxiety is nothing but thoughts**

- **I cannot control everything, and I am okay with that**

- **It doesn't matter what other people think of me**

- **I am living in the moment, and I love it**

- **I am safe**

- **I am in control**

- **I trust myself**

- **I inhale peace and exhale worry**

- **One day, one thing, one moment at a time**

- **The past and future doesn't exist, all I have is now**

- **This too, shall pass**

Some of these will really work for you, so you should explore them and feel which ones resonate the most. Use them daily.

Activities for positive self-talk

1. Before you go to bed, write down one thing you like about yourself, and stick it on your bathroom mirror. In the morning when you wake, let that one thing be one of the first things you see, to start your day well.

2. Make a shopping list, ensuring to add healthy fruits and vegetables that you love. On the list, write down one reason why you deserve to eat well for each item of food you add to it. You're consciously telling yourself that you deserve good things.

3. Think of one positive affirmation. If you need to, search online for them and pick one that you're drawn to. You can also make up your own. Write it down and take a photo of it, then add it to your phone's home screen. You'll see it every time you look at your phone.

Chapter

BUILDING HEALTHY RELATIONSHIPS AND SUPPORT SYSTEMS

nxiety recovery is not a sprint. You won't set off at 8 am and end up a totally relaxed, anxiety-free person by 8:15. With all the will in the world, there is no overnight fix. With that comes one reminder you must take comfort and reassurance in:

Anxiety recovery is very possible.

I need you to understand that, because any type of recovery and healing isn't linear. You don't put it on a line and follow it until you reach the end. You will experience days more challenging than others, and the more you push your comfort zone outward, the more you may want to run to safety and hide.

To recover from anxiety involves conscious effort to keep going, and not give up. You'll probably want to some days, because all you've known, all that's been familiar to you is the burdening weight

109

of worry, and even if it's unhealthy, you will know it and recognize it.

Anxiety is fuelled by the unknown, so to be a worrier in itself is a comfort to those who know the feelings, the cycles and the outcomes.

It's not all on you, either. If therapy is something you want to seek so somebody can assist you with your thoughts and feelings, then go for it. If you need to visit your doctor and talk with them about how your symptoms seem overwhelming, then that's what they are there for. There are ways you can be supported so you don't have to feel you are walking your journey alone. Walking alone can lead to the feeling of being lost, which I know you don't want to feel, otherwise you wouldn't be reading this book.

Think of your recovery like a car - if you don't start the engine, you aren't going to go anywhere. Responsible drivers are equipped to drive a car, which means you need to now be responsible for your mental and physical health, and take the wheel.

Yes - the road isn't always clear, nor is it free from traffic and diversions, but you *will* reach the point where you are bigger than your anxiety, and the more you persist, the stronger you will become - weakening your worry.

Change Your Environment

Much of anxiety comes from the environment we place ourselves in. Have you ever noticed a room stiffen with tension the moment someone walks into it?

Unhealthy relationships entangle us all. They create that tension where they needn't, and can turn a happy, positive or even peaceful moment to be overtaken by utter toxicity.

I work regularly with a woman who said she used to literally go cold in the presence of a family member. She would find her hands and feet feel cold, and all she wanted was to wrap herself in a blanket and sit alone. All because they commanded attention wherever they went, and they would ridicule and torment anybody who allowed it. They were excellent at making others the butt of their jokes, and seemed to get off on making others miserable.

What does that mean for the average person with anxiety?

It means they resume that constant state of fear - what is going to happen next? *Will I be brought into this? Everything was so cheery until they came along, and now I feel like I want to run and hide. They make me feel terrible.*

Why should anybody make you feel terrible? Why should you be in an environment that is detrimental to your anxiety? Surely you want people around you to lift you up, encourage you and make you feel at ease, rather than those who apply pressure in such a constantly acute way.

Reducing contact with those who make you feel this way is an option. It may not always be possible, but it is a way of cutting the times you feel the way you do around them, which will improve your overall feelings towards the situation. It's not for me to tell you what to do, but if reducing contact is helpful to you, then it's something you can consider, as many people in similar situations have done.

It is difficult to reduce contact with work colleagues, so if work is an issue, you could look at applying those strict boundaries discussed previously. Focusing on the people you *do* get along with and switching off mentally as much as possible is key, especially when you don't have a choice.

Recovery and healing from any mental illness sometimes involves looking at your existing relationships, and noticing if anybody within your environment is feeding your worry and fear. Harmful behavior that derives from toxic relationships is enough to impact anyone's mental health, but if you are wired for anxiety, you are only going to see that increase in the presence of those with negative intentions and traits.

Signs of toxic relationships include:

- Feeling demeaned, criticized or unsupported

- You don't feel your best self around the person, such as you withdraw or turn into a bit of a gossip around them

- You get the feeling of walking on eggshells

- You feel blamed a lot of the time

- You feel devalued - by giving more than you get

- You don't feel your needs are being met

- You apologize to them a lot

- Your heart starts to race around them - they make you feel uncomfortable

Toxic people are unwilling to change - so it is left to you to take control.

Activity

If you can answer more than five of these questions about that potential toxic person in your life, the chances are they *are* toxic. The more 'yes' responses, the more toxic their behavior is likely to be.

1. Does there seem to always be drama around this person?

2. Do they always moan about other people to you?

3. Do you have a niggling feeling of discomfort around them?

4. Do you feel supported by them?

5. Do you feel listened to when you talk?

6. When you are with them, do they make you feel small or criticized?

7. Do you trust them?

8. Do you feel your emotions are in check when you are around them?

9. Do they boost your self-esteem?

10. Do they like/love you for who you are?

These questions are reflective and are meant to help you decide for yourself how much positivity these particular people bring to your life.

Establish healthy boundaries

It's safe to say that you aren't going to be able to avoid every person who makes you feel uncomfortable or who raises your anxiety levels to an unhealthy and constant level. Learning how to be around those people without compromising your mental health is imperative, and in times like these, boundaries are necessary.

As toxic people come with an intent to undermine you, you equally have the power to take that power away from you and give it to yourself.

What does applying strong boundaries feel like?

Boundaries give you the freedom, time and focus to put yourself first, and to keep your space safe from harm or toxicity. If you create a space that feels this way, you can divert far more focus to healing and how you *want* to feel.

When you first start applying boundaries, you will often be met with resistance. People aren't used to this version of you who says no, or who isn't at the beck and call of somebody. They won't be used to you asserting yourself and acting in accordance with your own values and beliefs, and, here's the cracker - if you stop 'people pleasing' - those who benefited from it will feel shell-shocked. You were once someone they could probably walk all over, and now they can't get to you because your boundaries are in the way.

Growth and healing is far more achievable with boundaries in place, because you no longer have their behavior to disrupt your journey.

Examples of verbal boundaries can be:

- *"I disagree with this."*

- *"I would like it if we could just agree to disagree at this point."*

- *"I won't be able to do that right now."*

- *"I am an adult, and I can make my own decisions."*

- *"I have my reasons and they are personal to me."*

- *"As an adult, I am not intimidated by you."*

- *"I am not prepared to discuss this any further."*

Other boundaries can look like:

- *Seeing that person less.*

- *Offering little information about yourself to them to protect you.*

- *Being polite and necessary, but not overly friendly.*

- *Creating a frame of mind that allows you to stand your ground in their presence.*

- *Letting go of the need to always be right for the sake of your inner peace.*

- *Asking for space when you need it.*

- *Leaving situations where you feel disrespected or not listened to.*

- *Simply being true to yourself and your limits.*

- *Remembering you have the right to change your mind if you want to.*

- *Prioritizing yourself.*

Activity

I've mentioned values in the book, and given you some opportunities to think about your own.

Now - it is time to think about how much you specifically value your well-being.

1. Take some time to think about what you think well-being means to you.

2. Write down any ways in which this particular toxic person is overstepping your boundaries. You can do this by thinking about how they make you feel and what they do or say to make you feel that way.

3. Write down ways you can implement stronger boundaries. Do you want to switch off or mute notifications from that person? See them less? Say no more, without apology?

4. Spend some time thinking about yourself and how you don't have to be treated like this. Use this activity and time to empower yourself rather than feel guilty about what you're doing.

Create support systems

What does a support system look like to you? When I think of support systems, I think of a collection of people who add essence to my life. I think about those who improve my mental health, encourage me to be the best version of myself, and who I can rise in mood and empowerment with.

A support system can consist of whoever you want, but the key in keeping them close to you is how much trust you have between you. This is about identifying those you feel are loyal and honest with you, as well as offering you guidance and support when you need it the most.

You, too, can be a part of somebody else's support system, and that's what creates this network of mutual understanding and love between us all. Having someone to rely on is so underrated, and in this day and age where everyone seems to be busier than ever, to still make time for what really matters is crucial to our combined well-being, but for those with anxiety, it's even more important.

But how can I build a support system?

It's not always better to work on yourself alone or isolate yourself. Support systems can be built by looking at who is currently in your life and choosing those you are drawn to the most. Who matches your energy? Who seems to always have your back, no matter what? Who will cheer for you when you are winning and pick you up when you feel down? Who matches your effort to maintain that connection?

If you feel you lack a support system, it's never too late to make friends and find your 'people.'

- *Try joining a sports or dance group to find new friends*

- *Look for local exercise classes where people on your wavelength might be found*

- *If you are a parent whose child attends activities, try getting to know a few parents a little more*

- *Look for ways to be out and about, even if it's a walk in a park where you might get to know another regular walker*

Any situation where you want to meet new people, you have to put yourself out there. They won't come knocking on your door.

Battles with mental health can feel like a complete uphill battle. Your own challenges make you feel like you either don't deserve your own support system, or try to prevent you from building one of your own. I'm here to remind you (not tell you, because somewhere inside your mind, you already know) that you are worthy. You're worthy of being cared for and loved, and your experiences thus far may not be in line with that fact, but it's still true.

Support systems offer a positive influence on us all. They give us as humans what we are intended to do - connect. We aren't supposed to fight alone, and we aren't meant to suffer alone either.

If you feel you lack a support system, start anywhere. If it is a therapist to start with, then so be it if it is an online support group, fantastic. Recruit who you need to, and identify those who are always there - a constant to you - and perhaps you to them.

There is a level of combined strength and belief that comes from saying, 'I'm not okay.' If you have a safe network of people you can offer that to, you are far more likely to find your worthiness amongst their support for you.

Remember:

The brain can work against you when you are at your most isolated and vulnerable. Highlighting your weaknesses, it can try to reiterate everything negative you think about yourself. Support systems help you fight that.

Trust is a huge part of belief that there are good outcomes to your anxiety, so keep those you trust close to you, and allow their strength to travel to you on those days you need it.

Activity

The next time you feel as though you need someone to talk to, I want you to think about the first person who comes to your mind who always makes you feel better.

1. Write down a little bit about them.

2. Who are they? How long have you known them?

3. How do they make you feel better?

4. What traits do they have that ensures a strong connection and level of trust?

5. Identify them on paper, and begin to see what a support system looks like in front of you.

This will help you in the future, as you can spot similar people and find comfort in the similar traits they also carry.

Chapter

8

IT'S A JOURNEY

There are a number of solutions out there that offer a 'quick fix.' You can drown your sorrows, or turn to equally unhealthy habits, but when it comes to your mental health, in your case your anxiety, there is no quick fix available.

Mental health journeys rarely begin and end when you plan. You can't set a date to say, 'that's when I will be healed!' - all you end up doing is setting yourself up for disappointment which in turn reinforces the negative thoughts and beliefs you are trying to battle.

Journeys have their ups and downs. Some day you might wake up thinking, 'what am I doing all of this for? It's pointless.' Other days will be more positive, where you can begin to see and *feel* real change.

Approaching your anxiety like a journey you need to undertake will help you build resilience as you move through it. Perceiving it simply as 'something you need to overcome' is only going to get you so far. You need to be aware of what's ahead. You need to actively *know* not every day is going to go the way you hope it will, and never underestimate the good days or moments, because they are to be celebrated.

The aim of any journey is to know yourself a little bit better than you did the day before, and to accept that it may be something you are always embarking on, rather than a point where you can say, 'here I am, I've arrived!'

Journeys are often eased by:

- The desire for change in your life

- Asking for help

- Coming up with a plan to treat your anxiety

- Applying hard work

- Never thinking of a destination, rather looking to improve

Getting started on your journey can feel like a moment you want to mark. I'll give you one piece of advice, though - don't wait for a cue - just get started.

- Build your own awareness of anxiety

Learn about yourself and why you think the way you do. This book can be read more than once, so you can always refer back to it when you need to.

- Find a counselor if you need to

Someone you feel comfortable sharing things with is going to help you feel as though you have a reason to let go of all the worry you hold in.

- Seek people who can support you and check in on your progress

Ask a trusted friend or family member to check in with you and see how you're doing. If you have intentions, they can be followed up with a simple query, call or text to ensure you're on track.

- Set expectations that are realistic

Charging ahead and assuming you're going to be all better in a few weeks or months isn't something you want to set yourself up for. Give yourself permission to feel, to grow, to heal. Be aware that quick fixes are never permanent and can lead to further problems down the line.

Consider your journey well, and know that:

- It takes courage to be vulnerable, so find yours

Vulnerability means to stop covering a feeling up because you don't like how it feels to expose it. Allow it to be. Allow your emotions to meet the air surrounding you, and sit with them, even if it feels uncomfortable. In the discomfort, you will find strategies to allow acceptance.

- You need to trust the process

Trusting the process is a huge part of embarking on any journey, because you cannot prepare for it in any way. Journeys are unknown, and too many people assume that to be something scary or negative, but in fact, it can be beautiful if you let it. Trusting that everything is going to unfold for the greater good will give you exactly the kind of strength you need to feel loved - not by anybody else - but by yourself.

Keep going - and never stop. Your progress isn't measured by miles, but in the effort it took to try.

This takes patience.

Be Patient

Patience is a huge aspect of your journey of anxiety recovery. If you have a bad day or even week, it'll be all your strength to not throw the towel in altogether and say, 'I've had enough, I wasn't meant for healing from this!'

It won't always be difficult. You'll have beautiful days where you can look back and say, 'I handled that totally differently to how I would have six months, or a year or more ago.' You will notice your well-being improve, but this all takes a great level of patience.

Patience derives from the acceptance that the big changes to your mental health do not happen overnight. Looking at other people who are going through something similar to you and wondering why *you* aren't letting go of those old habits yet, or why *you* still seem to have negative thoughts that prevent you from moving forward. Who's to say it's a race? Journeys are not about competing, they are about experiencing.

Anxiety and patience can be two concepts that don't meet very well, but once you get working on being patient in your journey of recovery, the more you will adjust. When you think about anxiety, it's a disorder that wants answers now. Do you feel nervous about something? You want it to be over now. Do you wonder what tomorrow will bring? You want to know now.

Patience is the opposite to anxiety, because it involves waiting to see how life and times naturally unfold. Patience is to know that what will be, will be, and you will know what that is when the time is right. Patience is being tolerant of problems, delays, or the unexpected. It is to wait without anxiety or annoyance. It is finding the restraint within you to say, 'We will just have to wait.'

So, when it comes to the journey you're undertaking (you have started it, even if you don't feel you have - reading this book is proof of that), you should hold that patience close to you, because there will be moments you will actively need to remember that not everything can be fixed all at once.

Have Faith

Much of your journey through discovering, identifying and recovering from the anxiety you have been going through, is to hold onto faith. Faith makes everything possible; it changes a challenge into a moment you can learn and adapt for the future, rather than slip back into your old, worrying ways. Results are a direct product of your effort, and some people like to see their results often, to keep them motivated. What might that look like to you? It may not feel totally fearful if a job interview opportunity arises.

You should use this book, these words, that feeling you get from knowing that healing is possible to fuel you. You *can* go from surviving to thriving, if you believe in the concept of reframing those day to day moments, and turn them into something magical, uplifting and positive.

In truth, thoughts aren't facts, and it takes patience to figure that out and sit with that in the journey of healing from worry.

Only you can experience your journey, and only you can come out stronger at the other end.

If you can learn to be patient in this, you can learn to:

- Develop a healthy attitude, and know that being so can make you more productive. Accept setbacks, and allow what will be, to be.

- Have a greater sense of gratitude by focusing on what *is* happening, rather than what you imagine to happen in the future. Focusing on what is good leads to feelings of good within you.

- Maintain and transform relationships by preventing yourself from becoming annoyed or irritated by what's going on. Slowing down and untying that hasty decision-making aspect of your anxiety will free your mind. Impatience is too inward, and it's chaotic when too much becomes inward. Allow the free flow of waiting.

- Slow down -smell the roses! If you have heard of that phrase, you can tune into it by letting patience become your mantra for life. You might even get some of that deep breathing in as well.

- Think a little more productively. Your thoughts will help you manage your emotions, and this is how patience is developed. Look at the big picture, not just the *right now*. Nothing is always right or wrong; it's all subjective and changing.

- Choose better. Patience is something we can all *choose* to feel. It's a choice to get wound up or frustrated, but it doesn't have to be that way. You can consciously say to yourself, 'I'm going to choose to relax through this process,' or, 'I will adjust my expectations for this.' Changing your thoughts eventually has a change in your entire brain chemistry.

- Surrender to the now. Impatience derives from trying to control something that is out of our control. We become frustrated because we can't see that we are powerless, or rather, we don't like to admit we are.

- Make you feel physically healthier. Letting go and becoming patient in your own self will rid you of any of the negative feelings associated with impatience. It is truly a gift to feel this way, and it can work for you.

To choose patience is to choose wisdom, and patience is going to heal you.

Keep a journal

There's no better way of being able to reflect on any healing journey than to journal. Keeping a journal has *so many benefits,* not least keeping your mind clear whilst you tackle the challenges and adventures along your way.

Journaling is like a sieve, because it helps you sort through everything you're feeling, some of which will be pretty complex. Anxiety has many layers, and sometimes, the only way to find and separate those layers is to have everything written down. You put all your thoughts and problems down, and you can literally feel them begin to be sorted before your eyes.

Moreso, journaling is a way of helping you visually notice your emotional patterns over time. The day you start to journal will be the time you look back on in weeks or months to come, and you can have those 'eureka' moments where the puzzle pieces begin to fall into place.

Generally speaking, journaling is like talking to yourself. It can make everything feel less overwhelming, which can take away the intensity of what you're experiencing. That level of calm and clarity can be reached, and it's easier than you think.

The benefits of journaling include:

1. Being in the moment

Your journal is like a mirror. To be looking at what you are feeling as it stares back at you is to truly be present.

2. Improving your emotional well-being

Your journal can't talk back to you, so whatever you write in it, it is going to allow you to do so. Having this special permission to be as honest as you can will help lift your well-being.

3. Helping you with your memory

You won't remember every little thing you write, but as you are able to reflect back on previous days, you can piece your memories together, helping you form stronger ones in the future.

4. Help you to problem-solve

What journaling can offer is a fresh perspective. As you read what you write, you can look for the solutions within your words.

Activity

How you can get started with journaling:

1. Grab yourself some supplies

Most importantly! You need a book you feel happy and comfortable writing in, and a good pen you can rely on to hold with ease. Whatever makes you happy - even unicorns!

2. Find a space of calm and relaxation

Pull yourself away from the everyday distractions of life with a place of calm serenity. Somewhere, you feel safe and able to be as honest as you can be.

3. Make time

Just like you would set aside time for your favorite show, set aside time to journal. Make it an important part of your day that you treasure - a sacred time for reflection.

4. Start with a small prompt if you get stuck

These prompts can help you begin your journaling day:

"What can you say to yourself today that is kind?"

"What did you find tough today?"

"If I knew failure was impossible, what would I do?"

"What do I need right now?"

"How was my day?"

"What am I grateful for?"

"What made me anxious today?"

"What are my worries right now?"

"What lesson have I learned today?"

"If I could go anywhere right now, where would it be?"

"What do I value?"

Celebrate wins

Your wins through your journey of healing will be testament to your resilience throughout. You only fail if you stop trying, so to persevere and create small wins for yourself, well, these are the moments you stop and absorb what is going on.

Consider wins to be like milestones, each one being an appreciative pause of reflection whereby you recognize your inner strength and how the outcomes to certain events have led to being positive enough to see yourself winning.

These wins are what will propel you forward and keep you going.

It is so easy, too easy for the brain to remember the negatives. I'm sure by now you are *acutely* aware of that! You look back and think of all the times you could have, should have, would have - but what about marking the occasions where you *did*. Where you said yes, and meant it, where you said no and meant it, where you were unsure, but you did or said it anyway.

Those moments are not to be forgotten, nor should they be. They are for you and you alone to fuel you to keep going.

Wins don't have to be big. They don't have to stop every person in their tracks, nor do they have to come tied with a bow for all to gasp at. Wins are personal to you. A win might be a boundary placed. A win might be going for that walk to shake off your negative thoughts. A win could be deciding to keep yourself busy when those negative thoughts start creeping in. A win is consciously doing something for yourself that is positive and *owning it.*

I wrote something for you when you feel you have won, and I'd like you to read it when you do, to reaffirm the celebration behind your success.

I celebrate the victories in my healing journey.

I recognize that not every step is easy, but I celebrate the times I overcome something I previously struggled with.

I am deserving of positive feelings, and I know that wins can be big or small.

I find motivation and strength in this win because it will lead me to another along my path.

I am conquering thoughts, feelings, and beliefs that once felt impossible to navigate. I do so with curiosity and an open mind because I know some things don't always go my way.

I am accepting of any win, big or small, because it is another step in my healing journey, and each step forward is a step where I become wiser and more knowledgeable.

Each time I overcome a challenge, I am led to the priceless belief that I can change and control my feelings. This means I can create positivity and self-awareness. This means I am far more capable than I ever gave myself credit for.

I am someone who matters, but I am who matters the most to me.

Reading and understanding these words will come more naturally to you as time goes on, but those wins - they solid never, ever be underestimated, because they are what will give you your power back.

If you ever feel yourself backing down from celebrating wins, remember that the celebration of the win keeps you motivated for the next time. Beating yourself up if you don't is not an option.

How might you celebrate your wins?

Celebrating small victories can look however you want them to look.

You can:

- Write down how you feel when you feel at your best

- Have a celebratory mantra ready - *I have got this!*

- Tell a trusted and encouraging friend or family member

- A little self-care - do what you love

- Take a personal day just for you

- Look at yourself in the mirror and smile - heck, even high-five yourself!

Celebrations aren't something we do nearly enough of. If we are to succeed and keep going with momentum under our wings, we are to realize that celebrations are what encourage us to never stop - no matter what.

Avoid toxic positivity

Finding similarity with the words 'toxic' and 'positivity' might seem a little strange for you, after all, why would the two have anything in common? In truth, separately, they don't, but together, they do.

Toxic positivity is the belief that no matter how terrible a situation you are in, or how hopeless you feel over a situation, that you should maintain a positive mindset. This is *not* about never thinking positively or hoping things get better, it is the idea that all negative emotions or feelings should be ignored and/or rejected in favor of you painting on a smile and pretending everything's fine.

Toxic positivity is denial.

Toxic positivity is like wearing a mask.

Don't get me wrong, positive outlooks are a good thing. It will improve your mental health to see life sunny side up, but we all know that life doesn't flow this way constantly. Life isn't always sunshine and roses, and those difficult days should be marked too. They should be marked because they are all part of the process, and that includes all healing processes.

It's widely believed by many that healing is about positivity and repelling anything negative, but let me assure you, healing can sometimes feel messy and confusing. That's because you are processing all the years your anxiety was *bigger than you*, and in trying to make it shrink, you are looking at all the challenges that come with getting out of your comfort zone.

Let me give you some examples of toxic positivity to help put it into perspective for you.

- You lose your job, and somebody tells you 'not to worry,' or, 'look on the bright side, things could be worse.' As encouraging as they might seem to that person, they aren't validating your sadness and disappointment at you losing your job.

- If you encounter a break up, or loss of some kind, someone might say, 'I believe everything happens for a reason. It was meant to be.' Pain can't be something you dodge, so hearing this from somebody is almost like their attempt to hide or disguise your pain.

- If you feel sad, or are having a bad day, someone may respond with, 'To be happy is to choose to be happy.' This phrase implies that you are not allowed to feel sad, or that you are choosing to feel something negative rather than accept the emotion as part of a process. It's not your fault.

When you hear phrases or statements like these, they rarely mean anything other than a well-intended clutch at being sympathetic, but in truth, comments like these can be harmful to those who hear them. Sometimes, they have no idea what else to say in that situation to help or support.

Optimism is key

In the face of challenge, optimism is key. The idea that you can stay hopeful is very different from denying your difficulties altogether.

Reasons why toxic positivity is harmful

- **It can lead to feelings of shame**

If you are told to buck up, cheer up, or anything else that denies your feelings, you'll automatically feel ashamed of feeling the way you do. That shame comes from feeling as though your own emotions are unacceptable. If you are having a bad day, your feelings should be valid and respected.

- **It may ignite feelings of guilt**

What are you doing wrong if you aren't staying 100% positive throughout what is likely to be very challenging times? The true answer is absolutely nothing. Only the approach others may have with their toxic positivity is that you're doing everything wrong by not retaining an insurmountable level of false happiness.

- **It doesn't allow people to be emotionally authentic**

Toxic positivity is known to be one of the biggest avoidance tactics when it comes to emotions. It's like being faced with something overwhelming and stepping away from it. Why? Because those who promote it don't want to handle it; they don't wish to open the can of worms that comes with challenge. This can happen internally too, when we tell ourselves to 'chin up and forget the sadness,' all we do is push that sadness deeper inside of us, instead of allowing it to be released. There is no freedom in trapping our sadness.

- **It stunts emotional growth**

A crucial thought to remember is that any chance we get to deny our true feelings, we aren't growing. If something hurts, you cannot cover and protect that pain, because eventually, it's going to tire you out. Letting it be what it is is a chance for curiosity and deeper insight into yourself, and *that* is what healing is all about.

The goal with toxic positivity is to allow *all* feelings, not just the good ones. 'Good vibes only' sounds great, and almost positive, but it is a restrictive view on emotions, and how only the good ones matter or count.

What you can do to avoid toxic positivity

1. **Be genuine in how you interact with your emotions.**

When you feel sad or overwhelmed, it's human nature to want to 'pick yourself up' and ignore what you're going through. Whilst it's nice to have a positive outlook and think, 'this won't last forever,' it's imperative to sit in sadness for a while.

2. Accept, not judge

Don't try to fix yourself. Being sad doesn't mean you're broken. Feeling frustrated or having a bad day doesn't mean you have a bad life. Let it be.

3. Encourage yourself to feel everything

Express yourself if you are feeling frustrated. Go for a brisk walk, journal, dance it out, scream into a pillow if you need to! There are great ways to release what you're feeling, because the alternative is to keep it inside.

4. Seek support if you need to

Family, friends, whoever you love and trust to listen to you will be there for you if you let them. Support is vital, but more important is the response you need from them. You don't need to hear, 'just get on with it, never let your head drop, keep going' all the time because not all the time do we feel like keeping going. The key is knowing we aren't going to stand still and stagnate in our negativity forever.

5. Reach out to a coach or therapist

Therapists and coaches can help you lean into your bad days and figure out ways you can change your thoughts and beliefs, but they also help you understand how to manage the negativity too. It's like getting stuck in the mud; you can stand in it and say, 'I'm stuck,' or you can, step by step, get yourself out. For that you need the tools, and you can find them, because they're already somewhere inside of you.

Expectations

As you work through your journey, and build up your well-being, you're going to naturally have expectations. Certain things you'd love to do, feel, or no longer feel. You will know the direction you want to walk, and you'll have small goals that you complete along the way. On those days these goals don't quite work out how you'd imagine them to, own it. Own the feelings. Own when you sit and question what all this is for, because if you ask that question, you allow room for the answers to appear. Denying the question altogether, will deny your answers, and leave you unable to grow and move forward.

I want to personally wish you all the best for your healing journey. Every day is going to be filled with things to learn, unlearn or relearn. You will be overriding a lot of thoughts that have so far, in your eyes, kept you safe. The beliefs you have, the way you are always thinking ahead and trying to imagine scenarios before they've happened has been how you have protected yourself. You have protected yourself from allowing the natural flow of life, but now is the time to breathe and let go.

Be there for yourself. Show up every day, not just the good ones. Consciously remember that journeys are not a start and finish, nor are they a straight line to success. The messy days are the ones where you grow the most, and the good days should be celebrated. Knowing all of that - there are therefore, *no bad days,* because each day is one to acquire knowledge you didn't have before. You're not only learning about anxiety, you're also learning about *yourself.*

You are the most important person in your world, and it matters that you start your journey now.

That anxious person you've always known?

It's time to tell them they can leave now.

It's time to tell them that you have got this.

Strategies

The strategies written within the book are all purposely written to be doable for even the most anxious person. Whilst they can be a challenge to ignite because your mind is giving you a thousand reasons not to, they are there for you to be the starting point for a turn of direction.

There is *something* you can do, and if you see a strategy you can slightly change to suit you - then go for it! The doors are firmly open for you when it comes to finding new ways, and I know you can do it. If you need that encouragement or sign to start - this is it.

Strategies should be looked at as your exit plan, so use them as such, and make sure any strategies you have are empowering and used to create the version of you that you want to be.

Remember one last, very important thing…

If you feel out of control and as if your anxiety is not reducing, it is a wise idea to suggest you reach out for professional support. There is no shame in it; in fact, you would be one of many doing so if you did.

Seeking professional help is an empowering move, and a great way to take control of something that you haven't been able to thus far.

- do not use "positive thinking" as the only strategy. You cannot positively think yourself out of anxiety. Include research studies here

Anxiety affirmations for you to try

Sometimes, it's helpful to have something at hand ready to fire at yourself when you need a mental pick-me-up. These affirmations do just that.

It's okay to make mistakes

I am worthy of receiving love exactly as I am

I deserve to be treated with respect, love and kindness

There are so many people who care about and love me

It's okay to struggle on some days

It isn't how you fall, it's how you get back up

One day at a time, one moment at a time

I love the opportunities life is giving me

My inner voice is positive

I am blessed

Conclusion

> "Anxiety's like a rocking chair. It gives you something to do, but it doesn't get you very far." - **Jodi Picoult.**

I like to think of books as journeys of their own, and if they accompany somebody on theirs, then both journeys can form an unforgettable bond.

That was my aim for you, with this book; to bond you with your thoughts, and help you see how unhelpful they can be. It is interesting that a thought can become as strong as a fact in the minds of those anxious. Granted, sometimes we can't help but think ahead and wonder, but when that wonder turns to fear or assumption that opens doors for detrimental symptoms and consequences, something needs to be done about it.

You have learned to understand your anxiety, what triggers are and how your own affect you, and how your negative thoughts are to blame. It isn't easy to change those, and it isn't a miraculous overnight alteration to your mindset, but as you've learned, mindsets are not fixed, and you can program yours to be your open, freer friend, rather than a one vision set of beliefs.

Anxiety statistics revealed that you are one of literally *millions* of people who are currently suffering with anxiety. Those days you feel alone, you must understand that you are not. All the different ways it can and is affecting your life are being shared by people you both know, and don't know, but the difference is, you *can* do something to change that. You *can* take the steps to decrease the anxiety, and increase your confidence and positivity behind your thoughts.

Finding new thought patterns can lead to the reduction of overthinking, and that's where you can really begin to appreciate well-being as a concept, and how you can improve your lifestyle long term for great results.

There's a world outside waiting for you, and support systems to grow, maintain and lean on. The journey for you now is your own to carve and create, but let me tell you, there is an open door, and it is beckoning you to the edge of your comfort zone.

It isn't scary, it's exciting.

So - what are you waiting for?

Your life starts today.

Thank you

I want to take this time to personally thank you for finding, investing in, and reading this book. I wrote it because I want to make a difference in the lives of people who feel they don't see or have a way to rid themselves of their anxiety.

If you find the book useful, please take a few moments to leave a review of the book and how it helped you. That would be amazing.

Thank you so much.

References

- *Anxiety Disorder | MQ Mental Health Research.* (n.d.). Www.mqmentalhealth.org. Retrieved January 15, 2024, from https://www.mqmentalhealth.org/conditions/anxiety-disorder/?gad_source=1&gclid=CjwKCAiAzJOtBhALEiwAtwj8tscrgcU7Vw4TiTQ7byMYgJIEnF4NNpCNrn0HRvQL4a97tmzaHsONEBoC2jkQAvD_BwE

- *Your brain when you're anxious.* (2020, April 6). Kids Helpline. https://kidshelpline.com.au/teens/issues/your-brain-when-youre-anxiou

- *Generalized Anxiety Disorder (GAD).* (2021, August 8). Www.hopkinsmedicine.org. https://www.hopkinsmedicine.org/health/conditions-and-diseases/generalized-anxiety-disorder#:~:text=GAD%20means%20that%20you%20are

- NHS. (2021, February 16). *Panic disorder.* Nhs.uk. https://www.nhs.uk/mental-health/conditions/panic-disorder/

- NHS. (2021, February 15). *Overview - Phobias.* Nhs.uk. https://www.nhs.uk/mental-health/conditions/phobias/overview/#:~:text=A%20phobia%20is%20an%20overwhelming

- NHS. (2021, February 16). *Social anxiety (social phobia)*. Nhs.uk; NHS. https://www.nhs.uk/mental-health/conditions/social-anxiety/

- Cherney, K. (2020, August 25). *Effects of Anxiety on the Body.* Healthline; Healthline Media. https://www.healthline.com/health/anxiety/effects-on-body

- *Worry and Anxiety: Do You Know the Difference?* (n.d.). Www.henryford.com. https://www.henryford.com/blog/2020/08/the-difference-between-worry-and-anxiety

- Holland, K. (2018, May). *What Triggers Anxiety? 11 Causes That May Surprise You.* Healthline; Healthline Media. https://www.healthline.com/health/anxiety/anxiety-triggers#triggers

- *When bad experiences trigger anxiety: childhood trauma and PTSD | Feature from King's College London.* (n.d.). Www.kcl.ac.uk. https://www.kcl.ac.uk/when-bad-experiences-trigger-anxiety-childhood-trauma-and-ptsd

- Stetka, B. (n.d.). *How the Brain Purges Bad Memories.* Scientific American. https://www.scientificamerican.com/article/how-the-brain-purges-bad-memories/

- Paul, M. (2015, August 17). *How Traumatic Memories Hide In The Brain, and How To Retrieve Them.* News Center. https://news.feinberg.northwestern.edu/2015/08/17/how-traumatic-memories-hide-in-the-brain/

- *Psychological Effects of Unhealthy Relationships*. (2023, September 29). https://compassionify.com/psychological-effects-of-unhealthy-relationships/

- Pedersen, T. (2022, April 28). *Triggers: What They Are, How They Form, and What to Do*. Psych Central. https://psychcentral.com/lib/what-is-a-trigger

- *Tips to Cope With Things You Can't Control*. (2022, March 24). Psych Central. https://psychcentral.com/blog/coping-with-what-you-cant-control#control-fallacy

- sevenmindsets. (2015, March 2). *Fixed Mindset - 3 Ways It Holds Many of Us Back*. 7 Mindsets. https://7mindsets.com/fixed-mindset/#:~:text=Fixed%20mindset%20thinking%20hinders%20risk

- *Unhelpful thinking styles*. (n.d.). Www.healthywa.wa.gov.au. https://www.healthywa.wa.gov.au/Articles/U_Z/Unhelpful-thinking-styles

- admin. (2019, December 3). *How to Reframe Our Story to Create a Better Life*. Terri Kozlowski. https://terrikozlowski.com/story-reframing-is-a-tool/

- *How to Stop Catastrophic Thinking: 6 Ways*. (2021, October 27). Psych Central. https://psychcentral.com/blog/catastrophic-thinking-when-your-mind-clings-to-worst-case-scenarios

- Straw, E. (2022, January 5). *How Shifting Your Attention Can Be the Cure for Anxiety*. Tiny Buddha. https://tinybuddha.com/blog/how-shifting-your-attention-can-be-the-cure-for-anxiety/

- *How To Stop Caring About Things You Can't Control |
  BetterHelp*. (n.d.). Www.betterhelp.com.
  https://www.betterhelp.com/advice/stress/how-to-stop-caring-
  about-things-you-cant-control/

- *Mental Filter: A Cognitive Distortion*. (2022, September 7).
  Mental Health Center Kids.
  https://mentalhealthcenterkids.com/blogs/articles/mental-
  filter#what-is-mental-filtering?

- *How Anxiety and Assumptions Work Hand-in-Hand*. (n.d.).
  Coastal Therapy Services, LLC. Retrieved January 23, 2024, from
  https://mainecoastaltherapy.com/blog/how-assumptions-and-
  anxiety-work-hand-in-hand

- *Cognitive Restructuring: Techniques and Examples*. (2020,
  February 4). Healthline.
  https://www.healthline.com/health/cognitive-
  restructuring#:~:text=Some%20people%20find%20journaling%2
  0helpful

- Pelechowicz, S. (2017, February 21). *How to Break the Bad
  Habits That Hold You Back in Life*. Tiny Buddha.
  https://tinybuddha.com/blog/how-to-break-the-bad-habits-that-
  hold-you-back-in-life/

- *Jay Shetty ON 7 Ways to Let Go of Bad Habits | Blog | Jay Shetty*.
  (n.d.). Www.jayshetty.me. Retrieved January 23, 2024, from
  https://www.jayshetty.me/blog/jay-shetty-on-7-ways-to-let-go-of-
  bad-habits

- *Rumination.* (2021, March 15). The OCD & Anxiety Center. https://theocdandanxietycenter.com/rumination/

- *How to stop ruminating.* (n.d.). Priory. https://www.priorygroup.com/blog/how-to-stop-ruminating

- *10 Tips to Help You Stop Ruminating.* (2018, May 24). Healthline. https://www.healthline.com/health/how-to-stop-ruminating#what-is-rumination

- Adler, F. (2016, March 10). *The Thinking Trap that Can Derail Your Goals.* DoTheThings. https://dothethings.com/thinking-trap-overthinking-derail-goals/

- Suni, E. (2020, December 10). *Anxiety and Sleep* (A. Dimitriu, Ed.). Sleep Foundation. https://www.sleepfoundation.org/mental-health/anxiety-and-sleep

- British Heart Foundation. (2018, August 8). *Sleeping tips.* Bhf.org.uk; British Heart Foundation. https://www.bhf.org.uk/informationsupport/heart-matters-magazine/wellbeing/sleeping-tips

- World Health Organization. (2023, September 27). *Anxiety disorders.* Www.who.int. https://www.who.int/news-room/fact-sheets/detail/anxiety-disorders#:~:text=An%20estimated%204%25%20of%20the

- *50 PTSD Statistics & Facts: How Common Is It?* (n.d.). Www.goldenstepsaba.com. https://www.goldenstepsaba.com/resources/ptsd-statistics#:~:text=While%20estimates%20vary%2C%20it%27s%20believed

- *Grow Your Mindset: Growth Mindset and Mental Health*. (n.d.). Growyourmindset. https://www.growyourmindset.co.uk/growthmindsetandmentalhealth

- *Why Do I Replay Conversations in My Head?* (2021, August 9). Psych Central. https://psychcentral.com/anxiety/rumination-replay-conversations-in-my-head#whats-rumination

- Mayo Clinic. (2022, April 28). *Relaxation techniques: Try these steps to reduce stress*. Mayo Clinic. https://www.mayoclinic.org/healthy-lifestyle/stress-management/in-depth/relaxation-technique/art-20045368

- *Self-care for anxiety*. (2021, February). Www.mind.org.uk. https://www.mind.org.uk/information-support/types-of-mental-health-problems/anxiety-and-panic-attacks/self-care/

- Rachel. (2020, April 20). *Black and White Thinking: 9 Easy Ways to Stop For Good*. Planning Mindfully. https://www.planningmindfully.com/black-and-white-thinking/#:~:text=and%20have%20patience.-

- MIND. (2019). *Self-care | Mind, the mental health charity - help for mental health problems*. Mind.org.uk. https://www.mind.org.uk/information-support/types-of-mental-health-problems/mental-health-problems-introduction/self-care/

- *24 Interesting Self Care Statistics for 2023 and Beyond*. (2023, July 29). Selfcarecabin.com. https://selfcarecabin.com/self-care-statistics/#:~:text=There%27s%20a%20recognition%20that%20self

- Saporita, N., & Institute, G. H. (2020, January 17). *Change Your Life in 45 Days Thanks to These Simple Self-Care Tasks*. Good Housekeeping. https://www.goodhousekeeping.com/health/wellness/g25643343/self-care-ideas/

- Ph.D, B. R. (n.d.). *Lower Your Risk Of Developing Anxiety By Almost 60% With Regular Exercise*. Forbes. https://www.forbes.com/sites/bryanrobinson/2021/09/12/lower-your-risk-of-developing-anxiety-by-almost-60-with-regular-exercise/

- *Exercise for Stress and Anxiety | Anxiety and Depression Association of America, ADAA*. (n.d.). Adaa.org. https://adaa.org/living-with-anxiety/managing-anxiety/exercise-stress-and-anxiety#:~:text=Scientists%20have%20found%20that%20regular

- Thomas, V. (n.d.). *Council Post: Five Ways To Set Boundaries With Toxic People*. Forbes. Retrieved January 31, 2024, from https://www.forbes.com/sites/forbescoachescouncil/2020/01/31/five-ways-to-set-boundaries-with-toxic-people/?sh=6503af6fd02c

- 59 phrases to help you set boundaries - PR Daily. (2021, August 23). *PR Daily*. https://www.prdaily.com/59-phrases-to-help-you-set-boundaries/

- Hood, J. (2020, February 3). *The benefits and importance of a support system | Highland Springs Clinic*. Highland Springs. https://highlandspringsclinic.org/the-benefits-and-importance-of-

- a-support-
  system/#:~:text=The%20definition%20of%20a%20support

- *Mental health*. (n.d.). Msf.org.uk. Retrieved January 31, 2024,
  from https://msf.org.uk/issues/mental-
  health?gad_source=1&gclid=CjwKCAiA_OetBhAtEiwAPTeQZ5
  OIGZuSVuuJa1q1kBPTtIZKGTrpXLR0StOFiHjAWk4DDAIX9
  QFFbBoCIZwQAvD_BwE

- Pindar, J. (2022, June 15). *Anxiety Statistics UK | 2022 Data.*
  Champion Health. https://championhealth.co.uk/insights/anxiety-
  statistics/

- *Understanding the mental health journey — and how to read the
  map.* (n.d.). Www.betterup.com.
  https://www.betterup.com/blog/journey-mental-
  health#:~:text=along%20the%20way.-

- *The Skill of Patience.* (n.d.). Columbia Metropolitan Magazine.
  https://columbiametro.com/article/the-skill-of-
  patience/#:~:text=Patience%20helps%20you%20to%20develop%
  20a%20healthy%20attitude.&text=Patience%20improves%20you
  r%20ability%20to

- *Journaling for anxiety: 15 prompts to help you release stress.*
  (2023, October 4). Calm Blog.
  https://www.calm.com/blog/journaling-for-anxiety

- Warrior, E. (2023, November 13). *Celebrating Milestones in
  Healing is a Recognition of Your Strength.* Medium.
  https://medium.com/@empathicwarrior/celebrating-milestones-in-
  healing-is-a-recognition-of-your-strength-

e9fe942b953a#:~:text=So%2C%20how%20can%20one%20celeb
rate

- Cherry, K. (2021, February 1). *Why Toxic Positivity Can Be So Harmful*. Verywell Mind. https://www.verywellmind.com/what-is-toxic-positivity-5093958

- Paulise, L. (n.d.). *5 Ways To Avoid Toxic Positivity And Support Better Those You Care About*. Forbes. Retrieved February 2, 2024, from

https://www.forbes.com/sites/lucianapaulise/2022/12/27/4-ways-to-avoid-toxic-positivity-and-support-better-those-you-care-about/?sh=7f4ac22a6d63